BOCKING DEANERY

Will of Aetheric of Bocking. Undated but probably A.D. 961-995. Canterbury, *Chartae Antiquae* B.2.

Bocking Deanery

The Story of an Essex Peculiar

by

ANN HOFFMANN

PHILLIMORE
London and Chichester

1976
PHILLIMORE & CO., LTD.,
London and Chichester
Head Office: Shopwyke Hall, Chichester,
Sussex, England

ISBN 0 85033 226 5

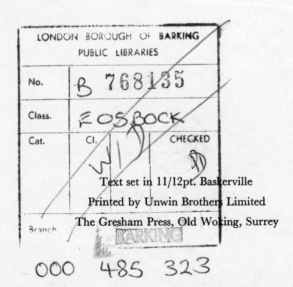
Text set in 11/12pt. Baskerville
Printed by Unwin Brothers Limited
The Gresham Press, Old Woking, Surrey

For Mollie and Freddie, who
entertained me on my visits
to Essex

CONTENTS

LIST OF PLATES

LIST OF FIGURES

ACKNOWLEDGMENTS

For permission to reproduce the illustrations in this book the author and publishers wish to thank the following:

His Grace the Archbishop of Canterbury and the Trustees of Lambeth Palace Library (Figs. 9 and 10).

His Grace the Duke of Atholl (Plates 12 and 13; photographer Alex C. Cowper).

The Dean and Chapter of Canterbury (Frontis. and Plates 1-4).

The Registrar of the Province of Canterbury (Figs. 11 and 12).

The Very Reverend Kenneth E. Wade, Rector and Dean of Bocking (Plates 5, 7, 20, 22, 25, 26, and Figs. 5 and 6; photographer, of Plates 5 and 20, A. F. Whybrow).

The Hon. Mrs. Derek Winn (Plates 15 and 16; photographer, Arthur Wright).

Mr. V. R. Coward and Mr. A. E. Evans (Plates 23 and 24).

Mr. A. E. Evans (Fig. 2).

Dr. F. G. Emmison (Plate 11).

Mr. A. F. Whybrow (Plates 5, 17, 18, 19, 20 and 21).

The British Library (Plates 6 and 10; photographers, R. B. Fleming & Co. Ltd.).

Essex Record Office (Figs. 3, 7 and 8).

Mary Evans Picture Library (Plate 9).

Radio Times Hulton Picture Library (Plate 8).

Trinity College, Cambridge (Plate 14).

Fig. 4 and 'Old Harkilees' on p. 72 are reproduced from *Braintree and Bocking* by M. Cunnington and S. A. Warner, 1906 (photograph by E. R. O.).

The dolphin badge on page 47 is reproduced from *Essex Review*, July 1926 (photograph by E. R. O.).

The 'View of Bocking' by W. Rothenstein, engraved by Walter & Cockerell, which appears on the dust jacket, is reproduced from the frontispiece to *Register of St. Mary's Church, Bocking, 1558-1639* by J. J. Goodwin, 1903 (photographer, N. Hammond).

FOREWORD

by

Col. Sir John Ruggles-Brise, Bt, C.B., O.B.E., T.D., J.P.,
H.M. *Lord-Lieutenant and*
Custos Rotulorum of the County of Essex

To one who is proud of his Bocking ancestors, Miss Hoffmann's invitation to write a Foreword gives particular pleasure. I used to enjoy reading the late Alfred Hills's Bocking articles in the *Essex Review*, and here is an immense wealth of new information about the parish whose fortunes for centuries have depended so much on the vagaries of the textile trade.

Bocking Deanery has its origins nearly a thousand years ago, when the Saxon King Ethelred confirmed a private gift of an estate at Bocking to Christ Church, Canterbury. Thus Bocking Church came under the Archbishop's jurisdiction, exempt from that of the Bishop of London, in whose diocese Essex lay. We all know that some of the great Essex churches, such as Thaxted, were built by groups of wealthy parishioners or affluent merchants, and this book contains a vivid account of those benefactors, many of them local clothiers, who helped to build and furnish St. Mary's Bocking, through the centuries.

The author, although not a native of the county, has dug deeply and skilfully into local, as well as national, records for her material. She has discovered a number of fascinating incidents in the lives of the various Deans who have resided at Bocking —episodes that will thrill and absorb her readers. Miss Hoffmann also tells the story of the Deanery house itself, the oldest part of which dates back as far as 1300, and brings it up-to-date with mention of the restoration recently carried out through the initiative and devotion of Mr. A. E. Evans. The house is now a private residence.

Bocking Deanery makes a welcome contribution to our Essex local history. It will interest all who enjoy reading about our past and should give pleasure to many people in the county and elsewhere.

AUTHOR'S NOTE

The idea for this book was first put to me in 1968 by Mr. A. E. Evans, at whose instigation extensive restoration work was then being carried out on the Old Deanery at Bocking. Of the many people who have given me help and encouragement during the research and writing, it is Mr. Evans to whom I am most indebted for his sustained interest in the project, even long after his own ambitious plans for it had to be dropped and ownership of the property had passed into other hands.

I should also like to express my gratitude to the present owner of the Old Deanery, Mr. V. R. Coward, for his generous contribution towards the cost of publication. But for his support this fragment of Essex history, necessarily of limited interest, would not have been an economic proposition so far as the publishers are concerned.

I am deeply grateful to The Very Reverend Kenneth E. Wade, the present Dean and Rector of Bocking, for putting at my disposal the papers in his possession, and for his constructive comments on my text; to Dr. F. G. Emmison, former County Archivist of Essex, for his help with documentation and suggested amendments to my first draft; to the staff of the Essex Record Office, Chelmsford, for their assistance with local records and illustrations; and to the Archivists of Lambeth Palace Library and Canterbury Cathedral Archives and Library for access to the old charters and other official documents relating to the Peculiar.

A former Dean of Bocking, Canon H. D. S. Bowen, received me most hospitably and has allowed me to make use of his notes on some of the earlier deans; Mr. Harold Joyce, churchwarden emeritus of St. Mary's, Bocking, has been a tower of strength, lending me his personal jottings on the history of the Church and Deanery, patiently answering my many queries and commenting on the draft typescript. For information on the structure of the house I have relied largely on notes prepared by Mr. Cecil A. Hewett. Miss E. M. McInnes translated several of the medieval

Latin charters for me, and Mrs. Pat Hodgson located some of the portraits.

Mr. S. M. Jarvis, Chelmsford District Librarian, helped me to obtain a print of the engraving used on the dust jacket, and my special thanks are due to Mr. A. F. Whybrow of Braintree, who not only contributed several pictures from his own collection but also took photographs of St. Mary's Church and the Doreward memorial specifically for this book.

For access to, and permission to quote from, private papers of the Murray-Aynsley and Oakeley families I wish to thank Mrs. Wilfrid Lloyd, the Hon. Mrs. Derek Winn, and Mr. Rowland Oakeley.

Mrs. J. H. Gerrard and Mrs. R. H. Sawyer were kind enough to give me their personal recollections of the late Dean Rogers.

I am also grateful to Professor Dorothy Whitelock and Cambridge University Press for permission to quote two short passages from *Anglo-Saxon Wills*.

Without the co-operation of all these people, this book would not exist in its present form. For the use that I have made of their material, as well as for any omissions or errors, I alone am responsible.

November 1975   A. H.
Eridge, Sussex

I

ORIGINS

A Thousand Years

The house stands on high ground, so screened by trees and foliage that even in winter you can barely glimpse it from the road. Where horses and riders once galloped boldly in and pony carts or elegantly appointed carriages sedately rolled, cars now make the same sharp turn on Deanery Hill, on the Panfield road out of Bocking, and drive through the gates and up the steep slope to the front door.

At once the visitor is attracted by the painted shield on the gable over the door: a silver cross on a blue ground between four dolphins. This represents the Deanery seal, a combination of the arms of the Priory of the Holy Saviour of Canterbury and the crest of William Courtenay, who was Archbishop of Canterbury from 1381 to 1396.

It does not need an architect to appreciate that here is no ordinary property. The very name, *The Old Deanery,* affords a substantial clue to its past. But why the arms of the See of Canterbury on a house in the heart of Essex? The answer lies in an ancient charter of the 10th century, still preserved in the Library at Canterbury Cathedral.

There have been many changes at Bocking since that time: from forest to farmland; from simple priest's hut to timbered Tudor hall; from an elegant mansion once the official residence of the deans to (only recently) a private house. If today the place seems to lack something of its former grandeur, we must remember that we live in a century that is less 'grand'. And that those who now drive in and out in their modern automobiles are no less a part of its history than the erstwhile deans and their ladies who used to pick their way in more leisurely fashion across these same lawns and down the Great Walk, or than their primitive heathen ancestors who lived by hunting in the nearby forests long before Christianity spread to Essex.

The documentary records of this unique house are scanty, but an attempt has been made here to piece together what is available in a chronological sequence. In the absence of written evidence, dates for the different stages of the house's construction and reconstruction must necessarily be partly conjecture backed by comparison with other Essex buildings. Compiled by a lay-woman for (it is hoped) the pleasure rather than the instruction of its readers, this book makes no claim to be a contribution to English church history: with so crowded a canvas there is space only to highlight the most notable events and personalities connected with the Deanery against a more lightly drawn sketch of the relevant age. The word 'Deanery' in this context should be taken as referring to the *house* rather than to the office or group of parishes under the jurisdiction of the Dean. How Bocking became a 'Peculiar' of the Archbishop of Canterbury, exempt from the jurisdiction of the Ordinary (i.e. the bishop of the diocese), is the turning-point of the story; a story that spans over a thousand years.

Early Inhabitants

Long before Bocking existed as a settlement, in fact long before the East Saxons came here and gave their name to the kingdom of Essex, man lived in this part of Britain. In those days the whole region was one vast forest. Few traces of prehistoric occupation have survived, although some remains of lake-dwellings, thought to date from the Bronze Age, have been discovered at nearby Braintree.

The site of the Deanery may once have been a prehistoric camp. Archaeologists have traced a footpath running obliquely up the bank alongside Deanery Hill which is similar to other paths found close to ancient settlements, and the theory has been advanced that the bank itself may be of artificial construction. Two recent occupants of the house noticed 'crop marking' in the grass during hot weather, and significant rubble has been found under the lawn beside what is now the ornamental terrace. The property was formerly enclosed by a ditch, now filled in, originally dug for fortification purposes.

The earliest known inhabitants of this region were the Trinovantes, a tribe of Alpine descent who lived here from about 500 B.C. up to the time of the Roman conquest. Basically a peaceful, agricultural race, they were later overpowered by savage Belgic invaders whose chieftain Cunobelin (Shakespeare's *Cymbeline*) adopted as his capital the old tribal town of the Trinovantes, renaming it after the war-god Camulos. It was from Camulodunum, now Colchester, situated conveniently on the estuary of the river Colne, that Cunobelin traded with the Continent, exchanging British slaves, cattle, iron and corn for wine and other luxuries.

The early Britons were a heathen people who lived and hunted in the forests round about, worshipping their own gods and the oak tree. Under the influence of the *Belgae* they learned to plough and farm the land. They also became skilled in the art of war, and by the time their red-haired Queen Boadicea led a revolt against the Roman oppressors in the year 61 A.D., the men of this neighbourhood were among her fiercest and most loyal supporters.

Throughout the Roman occupation of Britain, the district enjoyed considerable importance. Nearly a hundred years after the first unsuccessful invasion by Julius Caesar in 55 B.C., the Romans invaded again, this time under the personal command of the Emperor Claudius. They landed in Kent, crossed the river Thames at Londinium (London) in 43 A.D. and advanced swiftly north-eastwards to establish the first Roman colony in Britain at Camulodunum. The ancient British track from London to Camulodunum was adopted by the invaders and soon became one of the busiest thoroughfares in the land.

The Romans constructed a network of great highways, among them Stane Street, linking Camulodunum and Verulamium (St. Albans), and the road running north-eastwards from Londinium through Caesaromagus (Chelmsford) in the direction of Sudbury and Bury St. Edmunds. The junction of these two roads was the natural choice for a settlement: the town built on high ground lying between the Brain and Pant rivers which we now know as Braintree, called earlier 'Raines' or 'Branchetreu' (meaning 'town near a river'). Excavations suggest that there may have been a pre-Roman camp on this site. The Romans themselves certainly kept a huge hoard of money here, for quantities of coins have been unearthed near the road, at the point where today Braintree adjoins Bocking.

At this date there was no known settlement at Bocking. In any case, the Romans would hardly have established another town so close to their Braintree camp. But since they set up military bases at strategic positions all over the region, it is more than likely that their sentries had a look-out post here and that the Roman legions marched this way en route to and from Colchester.

It is not difficult to visualise the scene as it would have appeared to those sentries on Deanery Hill: still largely forested, apart from the low-lying agricultural areas and close-knit farming settlements; the township of Braintree on a hill to the south and beyond it the fortified military camps; the landscape intersected by two straight highways. With a little imagination you can almost hear the marching feet, see the sunlight glinting on shield and helmet, and recognise the harsh voices and clatter of armour as they set up camp for the night!

Roman rule lasted for 400 years. Then, following the Teutonic conquest of Gaul in the 5th century, the Romano-British found themselves not only cut off from Rome and all reinforcements, but had to defend their positions from vicious attack by the Picts in the north and the Saxons in the south and east. After 450 A.D., when the Roman legions eventually withdrew altogether from Britain, there came an influx of Jutes, Angles and Saxons, who between them established seven kingdoms: Essex, Wessex and Sussex, ruled by the Saxons; Kent, under the Jutes; and East Anglia, Mercia and Northumbria under the Angles, after whom the whole island was named.

Among these invaders, probably at some time during the late 5th or early 6th centuries, came one called Bocca, who chose to settle on the north bank of the river close to the old Roman township of Braintree.

Bocca

The East Saxons who sought to establish themselves in the Kingdom of Essex were quick to appreciate the importance of road and river communications. Suspicious of the Roman towns with their fine stone buildings, however, the newcomers, who were accustomed to building with timber and thatch, settled mostly in the low-lying areas a little distance from the existing townships. Bocca selected his site on the banks of the river Pant, at the point where it becomes the Blackwater, not far from the junction of Stane Street and the Chelmsford-Sudbury road.

It has been said that Bocca was a Viking and that he came originally from the Frisian Islands. But if he arrived in Britain as early as the 6th century, it is more likely that he was a Frisian, for the first Viking raids did not take place until the end of the 8th century. Like other Frisians of his time, he probably joined up with a group of Saxons who had invaded the Frisian Islands on their way from Germany to Britain. Alternatively he may have been a Viking who had invaded the Frisian Islands before embarking on his voyage across the North Sea, in which case he must have been one of the first of his race to settle in Britain.

Whatever his birth, Viking or Frisian, Bocca was definitely a brave sea warrior. It was no mean feat in those days to voyage as he did with his followers, in a long wooden boat hung with painted shields across that treacherous stretch of water, to found his *ing*, or family settlement, in the Saxon kingdom of Essex. He was of course a heathen and worshipped the sun on Sunday, the moon on Monday, and Woden and Thor, the gods of storm and thunder, on Wednesday and Thursday. We know little of this great adventurer, but his hamlet, 'the settlement of the people of Bocca' (old English Beocca), written in the earliest records as Boccinge, Boccinges, Bockinges, Bockyng or Boquhing, has flourished for almost 1,500 years.

Two alternative theories have been put forward by historians for the origin of the name 'Bocking'. One, that it is derived from the Saxon word *bōc*, a beech tree, and *ing* meaning meadow or pasture, has been demolished by one local historian on the grounds that beech trees do not grow in the clay soil of the neighbourhood. (There are nevertheless two old beeches at the Deanery.) E. Ekwall, in *English Place-Names in -ing*, confirms that this derivation is out of the question. The other theory, that the manor was *bocland*, or free land, held by a private owner by *boc*, or charter, has also now been dismissed by most writers.

In this book it is Bocca whom we honour as the founder of Bocking.

The Coming of Christianity

The next 300 years saw much unrest and fighting between the different kingdoms and between the Anglo-Saxons and the invading Danes. Christianity spread to Essex, and one by one the Saxon nobles were baptised into the faith. At some time during the first half of the 10th century, the lord of the manor of Bocking became a Christian and, in accordance with custom, built the first wooden church on his land.

The new religion had first reached Britain under the Romans, but early Anglo-Saxon invaders had driven the British Christians westward to Ireland and the Scilly Islands. Although Celtic missionaries such as St. Columba tried hard to spread the gospel of Christ eastwards again, they made little impact upon the heathen English until after the arrival of St. Augustine.

In the year 597 Pope Gregory sent Augustine to Kent, where the King was married to a Christian princess from Gaul. The missionary was received with much courtesy by King Aethelbert at Cant-wara-byrig (Canterbury), capital of the kingdom of Kent, and he was granted a site outside the city walls on which to found his monastery. The King himself was baptised, and he made Augustine the gift of his palace. Here, on the site of a church built by the Roman Christians, a new church was consecrated in the name of the Holy Saviour. Augustine became the first Archbishop of Canterbury and his church (later Christ Church) Canterbury Cathedral. Throughout the Anglo-Saxon period the city was the religious and cultural centre of the land.

Early in the 9th century the kingdom of the East Saxons fell under the rule of the West Saxon kings, the greatest of whom was Alfred. He ruled from 871 to 899. Shrewdly he purchased peace from the Danes in order to gain time to organise his armies, and ultimately he defeated the invaders, forcing their leader, Guthrun, to adopt the Christian religion and to divide the kingdom with him. Essex, together with the region north of the Thames, became *Danelaw,* under the rule of the Danes, while King Alfred ruled London and the south.

Alfred was a patron of learning, and scholarship flourished at his court. During his reign the first documented history of England, the great *Anglo-Saxon Chronicle,* was begun.

After Alfred's death, faced with continual hostility on the part of his Danish subjects, King Edward, son of Alfred, determined to conquer the Danelaw. Essex was one of the first parts of the kingdom recovered from the Danes, but even then was fraught with internal unrest instigated by pro-Danish sympathisers. Under a later monarch, Edgar, who reigned from 959 to 975, a policy of fusion and conciliation towards the Danes was introduced and the feudal system, by which a man owed loyalty to his lord, began to emerge. Together with his close friend, Dunstan, Archbishop of Canterbury, King Edgar continued his father's tradition of the monastic and literary revival.

England still suffered then from the menace of Scandinavian invaders. The Vikings who persisted in raiding the English coasts were quick to take advantage of the inability of a later king, Ethelred (nicknamed 'the Unready'), to organise properly the defences of his realm. The collection of *Danegeld,* the tax which had been levied sporadically since Alfred's reign to buy off the invaders, now became a regular burden, a task which fell increasingly to the lords of the manor. Huge sums of money were paid over to keep the Danish marauders at bay.

Much of the land was now administered by *ealdormen,* thanes appointed by the King to represent him in the shires. In Essex the most famous of these ealdormen was Bryhtnoth, hero of the great battle of Maldon fought, and lost, against the Danes in 991.

At this time there was alleged to be a conspiracy in Essex to receive the Danish king, Sweyn (known as 'the Fork-Beard'), and to put him on the throne of England. A thane of Bocking, Aetheric (sometimes spelled Aethelric or Ethelric, and known also as Aetheric Worthfulman), was implicated in this plot. If the accusation was true, it illustrates all too clearly the contempt which many Englishmen felt for the corrupt and inefficient rule of Ethelred. But in Aetheric's case the charge was never proved, in spite of an attempt to revive it after his death, and he did not, as many other Danish sympathisers did, forfeit his estates to the King. Had he done so, there would be no Bocking Deanery today.

The charge of conniving with the Vikings may have been
unjust as far as Aetheric of Bocking was concerned. The writer
of the Old English poem, *The Battle of Maldon,* records how
after Bryhtnoth had been slain by the invaders 'those who had
no wish to be there turned from the battle', while other more
loyal thanes fought nobly on:

> . . . Still in the van stood Edward the Long, bold and
> eager; he spoke vaunting words, how he would not flee
> a foot-space or turn back, now that his lord lay dead.
> He broke the shield-wall and fought against the warriors,
> until he had taken due vengeance upon the seamen for
> his lord . . . So too did Aethelric, Sigebriht's brother, a
> noble companion, eager and impetuous, he fought right
> fiercely, and many another. They clove the hollow shield
> and defended themselves boldly. The buckler's edge burst
> and the corselet sang a fearful song . . .[1]

Was this 'eager and impetuous' warrior who fought the Danes
'right fiercely' our thane of Bocking? We cannot be certain.
Aetheric was a common Saxon name, and by the time the
accusation of conniving with the enemy was revived, Aetheric of
Bocking was dead and unable to refute it. Sweyn was not
acknowledged as King of England until several years later, in
1013, and by this time Aetheric's lands at Bocking were safely
in the possession of the monks of Canterbury.

Aetheric of Bocking

Aetheric had inherited Bocking from his father. He also held
other freehold lands in Essex and Suffolk. Wherever his sympathies may have lain at the battle of Maldon—with the English
or with the Danes—he was above all a pious Christian. Throughout
his life he worshipped regularly at his little wooden church at
Bocking, and in the will he made before going off to fight
at the battle he bequeathed all his landed possessions to the
Church. The treasonable charge later laid against him may
have been trumped up by his enemies; he may, on the
other hand, simply have tired of paying out large sums of
Danegeld and having the invaders regularly plunder his lands

into the bargain. There is also the possibility that he was himself of Danish descent.

It is unlikely that he was a direct descendant of Bocca, although this cannot be ruled out. During a period of such disturbance it would have been remarkable for the manor of Bocking to have remained in one family for 400 years. And in his will Aetheric states that his father 'had before acquired' the land at Bocking, which would suggest that it was granted to him, possibly for services rendered to his King, or purchased by him, rather than inherited.

It was the custom of the Anglo-Saxon thanes who had been converted to Christianity to build private churches on their own estates, for the personal use of their family and servants. As has already been mentioned, these Saxons had no experience of building in stone—and in any case there was little of it available in this part of England. Their Essex churches, like their houses, were built of timber—usually tree trunks split into two, the bark outwards, the flat, cut side inwards held together by wattle and daub, and a roof of thatch. Aetheric's dwelling, near to where Bocking Hall now stands, must have resembled a log cabin, and standing close to it there would have been a smaller log cabin which served as the church. A tiny shack, rather like a mud-hut, housed the priest.

The Gift to Canterbury

No record has survived of the first Bocking church; we know only that one existed in 997, at the date of Aetheric's death. Probably it had been built by his father, and Aetheric would have been baptised there. He may also have married Leofwyn, his wife, in the same little church.

Like other Christian lords of the manor in his time, Aetheric resolved that his estates should eventually go to the Church. But he was a good husband, devoted to Leofwyn, and when he made the will his immediate concern was to provide for her so long as she lived. He makes no mention of family apart from his wife: either they were childless or by that date any sons they had may have been killed in battle against the Danes.

In the poetic phraseology of the age (the original will is in Saxon English), Aetheric 'makes known to whom after his days he grants the possessions which God has lent to him'. His two horses, his sword and belt, two round shields, two javelins and 60 mancuses of gold are to go to his lord. 'And I grant all that I leave to my wife for her lifetime; and after her death the estate at Bocking is to go to the community at Christchurch, for our souls and for that of my father who obtained it; all except one hide[2] which I give to the church for the priest who serves God there.' His estate west of Rayne is to go to St. Paul's, and various other lands to certain bishops for their churches; of these Aetheric singles out Bishop Aelfstan to 'protect my widow and the things which I leave her, and, if God grant him longer life than us, that he will help to secure that each of the bequests which I have made may stand.'[3]

Aetheric survived the battle of Maldon and lived for a further 30 years. Unfortunately for Leofwyn, by the time she was summoned to appear before King Ethelred and his Council at Cookham to present her widow's *heriot* (a render of certain goods or money to the lord on the death of a tenant) and to claim her bequest, Bishop Aelfstan also was dead. But she found a champion for her plea in Archbishop Aelfric.

The story is revealed in the King's charter[4] confirming the will:

It is shown here in this document how King Ethelred granted that the will of Aethelric of Bocking should stand.

It was many years before Aethelric died that the King was told that he was concerned in the treacherous plan that Swegn should be received in Essex when first he came there with a fleet: and the King before many witnesses, informed Archbishop Sigeric of it, who was then his advocate for the sake of the estate at Bocking which he had bequeathed to Christchurch. Then both during his life and afterwards, he was neither cleared of this charge, nor was the crime atoned for, until his widow brought his heriot to the King at Cookham, where he had gathered his council from far and wide. Then the King wished to bring up the charge before his council, and said that the Ealdorman Leofsige and many others were cognisant of the charge. Then the widow begged Archbishop Aelfric, who was her advocate, and Aethelmaer, that they would beseech the King that she might give her marriage-gift to Christchurch, for the sake of the King and all his people, to the end that the King would give up the terrible accusation, and Aethelric's will might stand; that is, as it says above, the estate at Bocking to Christchurch, and his other landed property to other holy places as his will specifies. Then may God repay the King! He consented to this for the sake of Christ and of St. Mary and of St. Dunstan, and of all the saints who rest at Christchurch, the terms being that she should carry out this and his will should remain valid.

This declaration was straightway written and read before the King and the council. These are the names of the men who witnessed this:

Archbishop Aelfric, and Aelfheah, Bishop of Winchester, and Wulfsige, Bishop of Dorset, and Godwine, Bishop of Rochester, and the Ealdorman Leofsige, and the Ealdorman Leofwine, and Abbot Aelfsige, and Abbot Wulfgar, and Abbot Brihthelm, and Abbot Aelfwold, and Aethelmaer and Ordulf and Wulfgeat and Fraena and Wulfric, Wulfrun's son: and all the thegns who were gathered there from far and wide, both West Saxons and Mercians, Danes and English.

There are three of these documents: one is at Christchurch, the second at the King's sanctuary; the widow has the third.

It must have been a solemn ceremony and an ordeal for Leofwyn. She herself died a few years later, probably in 1006, the year in which, according to the Canterbury cartularies, the manor of Bocking, togther with Bocking Hall on the island of Mersey (which had been Leofwyn's marriage dowry), came into the possession of the Priory of the Holy Saviour at Canterbury.

Years afterwards, when all monasteries were required to produce the title deeds to their lands and the original charter could not be found, a scribe wrote out from memory what he believed it to contain. There was little doubt in his mind as to how Bocking had been acquired, since every day the monks at Canterbury sang Mass for the repose of the two Saxon nobles, Aetheric and Leofwyn. He duly recorded that

In this year [1006] of the reign of King Ethelred Ethelric and Leofwine gave Bocking and Mersey for the support of the Monks.[5]

But he mistook the benefactors for two gentlemen, Leofwyn (or Leofwine) being both a man's and a woman's name, as Evelyn is today. Only when the original charter came to light much later was it realised that the gift had been made by a Saxon lord and his wife.

Another document of interest in the Canterbury Cathedral Archives is a *Bull de Privilegiis*[6] of Pope Alexander III (1159-81) to Herlewin, priest of the Holy Trinity, Canterbury and his brethren. 'Having taken their church under his protection . . .', the Pope confirms to them Bocking and its appurtenances, which they are to administer 'according to the rule of St. Benedict and the custom of the church'. They may choose chaplains to fill vacancies in the churches and present them to the Archbishop, and these are to be responsible for the spiritualities and temporalities. They are to have peaceful enjoyment of their rights.

So Bocking passed into the jurisdiction of the Archbishop of Canterbury, under whose control it has remained to this day.

II

ARCHBISHOP'S PECULIAR

Canterbury Monks

For the next 500 years, until Henry VIII saw fit to dispossess
the monasteries, the manor of Bocking was held by the Priory
and Convent of the Holy Saviour (Christ Church), Canterbury,
on behalf of the Archbishop. As lord of the manor, the Prior
had absolute authority; he wore a mitre and had a seat in
Parliament. In practice, his manor was administered by the
monks, a group of clergy who were nothing like monks in the
modern sense of the word. They were responsible for husbanding
the lands and for maintaining law and order in the name of the
Prior. By all accounts they did themselves very well, feeding off
the fat of the land and becoming more and more prosperous.
The chaplain, or parish priest, who was appointed by the Prior,
looked after the spiritual needs of the community.

Discipline within the medieval manor was strict. Offenders
against the law ran the risk not only of being brought before
the manorial court, but of cooling their heels in the pillory
and stocks which stood facing the church, roughly where
St. Mary's Parish Hall now is. This was once the site of a public
house called *The Kicking Donkey,* the present building, formerly
the Workmen's Hall, having been erected in about 1880. In the
Middle Ages there was almost certainly a whipping post nearby.
The monks are also said to have maintained a ducking-stool
beside the bridge for the correction of ladies of too verbose a
disposition, as well as a gallows at the Four Releet. The origin
of the name 'Four Releet' is not known, but the gallows may
have stood on a small triangular green at the point where the
road that runs through Bocking to Stisted crosses the old
Roman road from Braintree to Bury St. Edmunds. It is of
interest, although it does not prove the existence of gallows,

that when water mains were laid in Bocking before the First World War, a trench was dug across this green and the remains of a skeleton with a stake driven through its body were discovered at a depth of about 4ft. 6in.

Bocking was a natural stopping-place for pilgrims and other travellers, many of whom were glad of a night's rest and the hospitality offered by the monks. Archdeacons and bishops came at infrequent intervals, always with great ceremony and accompanied by a large retinue. And occasionally there were representatives of the King or Court messengers on official business, to be feasted and housed in a suitable manner.

Aetheric's wooden house and church were destroyed by fire during the early 11th century, and soon after the Norman Conquest of 1066 a second church was constructed on the same site. This new church was built of stone, with thick walls, small windows and squat pillars supporting round or semi-circular arches. All that remains of it are a few fragments of a cushion capital and the base of a shaft; these are now in the north aisle of the present church. At about the same time the monks rebuilt the manor house nearby, roughly where Bocking Hall now stands. Traces of its moated enclosure may still be seen.

The local priest at this date was probably more fortunate than most, for whereas in many other parishes that had passed into the control of the religious houses the incumbent's customary tithes had been appropriated by the monks and the priest was forced to live in very humble style, often barely able to keep a decent roof over his head, at Bocking the smallholding bequeathed in perpetuity by Aetheric at least provided him with a modest livelihood.

At Canterbury the original cathedral church of the Holy Saviour, founded by Augustine, had also suffered destruction by fire at the hands of Danish marauders. In 1070 Lanfranc, the first Norman Archbishop of Canterbury, began to rebuild the cathedral and to reorganise Augustine's monastery as a priory. Re-dedicated to the Holy Trinity, by which name it is mentioned in the *Domesday Book* as holding the manor of Bocking, the new building was itself burned to the ground a few years later. It was rebuilt soon afterwards by Archbishop William of Corbeil and consecrated as Christ Church in 1130.

Other Christian lords soon followed Aetheric in bequeathing lands to Christ Church. Some of the less affluent made smaller gifts, as one Richard Fitzsimon in 1226 gave 'to the honor of God and from Reverence to the glorious Martyr Thomas to the Prior of Christ Church Canterbury . . . Two Deer yearly to be delivered at Bocking on the translation of Saint Thomas whose hides are to be used for binding the books of the Precentor.'[7]

In the *Domesday* survey ordered by William the Conqueror and completed in 1086 it was recorded that

> BOCHINGES has always been held by the Holy Trinity as a manor and as four and a half hides; and there are two plough teams in the demesne. Then the men had 35 ploughs, now 29. Then 19 villeins, now 18. Then 25 bordars, now 44. Then 4 serfs, now 2. There is land for 300 swine, pasture for 60 sheep, 22 acres of meadow, and a mill. And there are 6 beasts, and 100 sheep and 54 swine. There belong to this manor now as then 2 hides in MERESAI: and there are there 1 plough on the demesne, and 1 plough belonging to the men, and 2 villeins, and 1 bordar, and pasture for 50 sheep. Then the whole together was worth 24 pounds, now 28.[8]

Some 300 years later, in the reign of Edward III, the manor was further enlarged by the gift of the manor of Bovington 'in the township of Bocking' and by two smaller grants on the part of local landowners.

Similar endowments made in other parts of England, and gradually all those pockets of land which passed out of private ownership into the possession of the Priory of Christ Church, Canterbury (thus outside the jurisdiction of their local bishop or archdeacon), became known as 'Peculiars' of the Archbishop and were administered by the Archbishop's appointed commissary, or Dean.

Peculiar jurisdiction was gradually abolished in the mid-19th century, under the Church Discipline Act of 1840 and subsequent Acts. The majority of the Peculiars were abolished in 1845, Bocking being one of the few that were retained. Although the title of Dean of Bocking is still conferred by the Archbishop of Canterbury, to whom the incumbent remains responsible, the office nowadays is one of honour and distinction in the Church and carries no jurisdictional prerogatives.

The First Deans

By the beginning of the 13th century the Priory of Christ Church owned so much land outside its own province that it was impossible for the Archbishop of Canterbury to maintain personal control over all the Peculiars within his See. Travel, although popular in those days of crusade and pilgrimage, was slow and extremely hazardous, especially in the winter months, so that it was not practical for the Primate to keep in regular touch with his clergy and the manor so far afield as Essex and Suffolk. He therefore adopted the custom of appointing a representative, sometimes—though not invariably—the incumbent of one of the parishes within the Peculiar, to the office of dean. The first recorded appointment is that of Peter de Wakering, who was made Dean of Bocking in the year 1232.

In its earliest form the title of 'dean' (from the Latin *decanus*) was a military term describing the chief or commander of a division of ten. It later came into ecclesiastical use as the head of 10 monks in a monastery, and the first Dean of Bocking may have been the spiritual head of the 10 monks administering the manor. It has been suggested that the Dean was so called because he was responsible for 10 parishes, six in Essex and four in Suffolk, that comprised the Peculiar. Most historians, however, list seven that came under the Deanery jurisdiction: the churches at Bocking, Stisted, Southchurch and Latchingdon in Essex (in the diocese of the Bishop of London), and the churches at Hadleigh, Monks Eleigh and Moulton in Suffolk (in the diocese of the Bishop of Norwich).

As the Archbishop's personal representative, the Dean had charge over all the spiritual matters in his Peculiar and was empowered to hold courts for the trial of ecclesiastical and moral offences.[9] Over the years the commissions of the Deans of Bocking have differed very slightly from one to another, some having more or less power to issue licences, to receive oaths of obedience, to make visitations, or to deal with matrimonial and tithe suits and to prove Wills.

In practice the holder of the office has always been the Rector of Bocking, but since 1572 the Rector of Hadleigh has with a few exceptions been appointed to serve jointly with him, an innovation first made by Archbishop Parker, and one which has earned the two incumbents the unique and popular title of 'the Twin Deans' and which is still carried on today. The Rector of Bocking is the senior Dean[10]

The fact that the Archbishop appointed a Dean of Bocking from the mid-13th century onwards did not mean that he ceased to take a personal interest in the Peculiar. From time to time he still came to see for himself how it was progressing. Such visitations, accompanied as they were by much pomp and ceremony, must have caused a rare excitement in the manor. When Archbishop Pecham came to Bocking in January 1280/1, the usual sentence of excommunication was published against all those impeding the Archbishop's visitation. It is also on record that Archbishop Islip, visiting the Peculiar in the summer of 1355, found that the Rector of Hadleigh had been absent from his cure for two years.

In 1366 it was the Dean of Bocking who cited the notorious John Ball, then living in Essex, to appear before the Archbishop Langham on a charge of heretical preaching. Ball, who was to be tried and hanged in 1381 as one of the leaders of the Peasants' Revolt, had already at that date been making inflammatory pronouncements from the pulpit advocating a classless society.

There was no Deanery house at this date, and it is unlikely that any of the early deans resided at Bocking. Some of them held high office elsewhere: John de Honesworth and Richard de Wynewyck were also chaplains to the King, and another early incumbent, who founded the first chantry at Bocking in about 1253, was Robert, Archdeacon of Stafford. When visiting the Peculiar the deans were probably entertained by members of the local nobility or lodged at the manor house next to the church and attended on by the Prior and monks.

The population of Bocking was increasing rapidly throughout this period and by the end of the 13th century had outgrown its tiny Norman church. The beautiful wrought iron hinges that have been preserved on the south doors of the present church, the woodwork of which has been restored, date from

1260 and are considered to be the finest example of 13th-century ironwork in Essex; they also suggest that a south aisle may have been added onto the nave at this time, to make the church cruciform in plan, as well as the chapels of St. Nicholas and St. Katherine, two saints of the Eastern church introduced into England by Crusaders returning sometime between 1095 and 1270.

Bocking had already come far since the days of Aetheric and his little wooden church. For more than 200 years the Prior and monks of Christ Church had administered his lands and considerably enriched his manor. The Deanery was now established as head of all the Archbishop's Peculiars in Essex and Suffolk.

Greater changes were on the way. Thanks to the foresight of Prior Henry of Eastry, a trade was to be developed locally that would later make Bocking a household word throughout the land and in many countries in Europe. The enterprising Prior, on one of his visits to the manor, had observed a derelict fulling mill that stood near to the ford. He decided to have it put in working order.

Medieval Manor

Henry of Eastry, from all accounts, was a most energetic, resourceful man. From the time he took office in 1285 until his death in 1331 he never ceased to rebuild, to re-organise, to embellish. To him Canterbury owes the beautiful arcading in the Cathedral Chapter House, and the Bell Harry Tower takes its name from the Prior who donated the original bell.

Whether or not he came frequently to Bocking, he seems to have taken a special interest in the manor and during his office initiated a number of new works here. A list drawn up in 1322 by one of the monks shows that in the years between 1290 and 1308 he provided for new hen houses, two granaries, a press-house for the preparation of verjuice or cider, a new gateway and a solarium. He also spent the large sum of £28 0s. 8d. on a new fulling-mill.

It was this last item of expenditure that was to have a most far-reaching effect on the hitherto basically agricultural community.

Bocking at this time was only one of a number of manors belonging to the Archbishop, but it was already producing a steady income for the Church, as is shown by a valuation prepared towards the end of the 13th century for a king's tenth (a tax on annual profits levied by the Crown):

Bocking

	£	s.	d.
Rents of assize	15	0	0
Rents of fowls, 41 @ 1d.		3	5
Barley-silver		16	0
Reliefs, Heriots and Amercements		6	8
Sale of Stock		16	0
Water Mill		10	0
Fruits of the garden and orchard		1	0
Dovehouse		1	0
Meadow, 4 acs...		8	0
Pasture, 5 acs.		5	0[11]
Arable, 342 acs. @ 4d.	5	14	0

Bocking as Prior Henry and his contemporaries knew it consisted of little more than church and manor house, with a group of cottages, and probably an ale house, stretching along both sides of the road we now call Bocking Church Street. The centre, or village square, was near the little wooden bridge over the Pant river. According to a charter of 1309,[12] the manor house was 'well and sufficiently built' and occupied a site of some five acres, including courtyard, garden and meadow. There was 'one dovecote there in good repair worth 4s. more or less . . . two mills, one a watermill for corn and another for fulling worth £7 6s. 8d. p.a. more or less.' The fishing in the millpools was worth 12 pence a year.

To the south of Stane Street, beyond the acres of well-kept arable, pasture and woodland surrounding the little town lay the Royal forest, protected by the old Norman law which had originally been established to indulge the King's passion for hunting. Close to where the Roman road from Braintree crossed the river—and probably at the point where a road now branches to Wethersfield—there was a hospice run by the monks for the lodging and refreshment of pilgrims and wayfarers. Next to it stood a chapel dedicated to St. James, the patron saint of pilgrims. The 'hospital of St. James, Branketre', as it appears in old records, has long since disappeared, and the *Six Bells* inn was later built on the same site.

It is amusing to read that those 13th-century pilgrims were just as uncertain as some people are today exactly where Bocking ends and Braintree begins! In their case the confusion is perhaps the more understandable, for those who journeyed from London to Suffolk and Norfolk to the shrines of St. Edmund at Bury and Our Lady of Walsingham would not have passed through the actual town of Bocking, which lay off the main road to the west. (Today we should call medieval Bocking a village, but in those days all small communities were 'towns'. In the 18th century the word 'town' became the accepted short form for 'market town'.) Southbound pilgrims wending their way from East Anglia to the shrine of St. Thomas at Canterbury most likely regarded the hospice as the entrance to Braintree, then renowned for a number of inns providing entertainment for travellers. The hospice was undoubtedly well patronised, especially when the river was in flood and the ford impassable.

Under the feudal system land was divided among tenants, who paid annual rents and were required to perform certain services to their lord according to the terms of their tenancy. At Bocking the monks of Christ Church represented the lord of the manor and held courts there on his behalf, to administer the lands and, when necessary, to punish offenders. The early court rolls containing records of the proceedings of the manor court were destroyed by local insurgents during the Peasants' Revolt of 1381, but from those later rolls that have survived we learn that the rebels had their lands seized by the lord of the manor and were obliged to appear before the court in order to seek re-enrolment of their tenure. For the new ratification they had to pay a fine of threepence each.

Cases of trespass were frequent. One tenant was fined 12 pence for allowing four pigs to stray onto the lord's stubble. Another was accused of appropriating part of the common land by erecting a hedge. A third, John Riseby, was alleged to have stolen doves from the manorial dovecote. In 1399 the court made an order seizing into the lord's hands part of 'le

Scolehouse' which had been built without licence on the lord's land.[13] Nor was the Rector immune from manorial jurisdiction. One incumbent, presented for stopping up a path used by tenants of the manor, was reprimanded by the court. He persisted in this offence and the following year was fined threepence. Two years later he was brought to court again, when the fine was increased to eightpence.[14]

Officials such as the reeve and the ale-tasters, of which there were two for each manor, were usually sworn in at the manor court. At Bocking there were also constables and night watchmen, who were empowered to arrest anyone who ventured abroad after the permitted time.

Some tenants were required to work for two days a week for the lord; others to cart manure for one day, or to render special annual services such as haymaking or harvesting. Every year a haymakers' feast was held, for which the lord traditionally provided a sheep to be roasted, three bushels of rye, a cheese and salt.

The great religious houses who owned estates at this period were able to put their farming on a profitable basis, fertilising and draining them as one unit, in a manner beyond the resources of the small landowner. By the close of the 13th century sheep farming, much encouraged by the growth of the cloth trade on the Continent, was rapidly gaining over arable farming in England. By this time, too, considerable quantities of corn and wool from Bocking were being exported to Flanders.

Bocking Cloth

Not all the wool produced at Bocking at the beginning of the 14th century was sold abroad, for the monks had prudently fostered a home trade in spinning and weaving that had been practised in the locality on a small scale since Saxon times. The cloth produced was coarse, but it afforded a profitable occupation especially during the winter months when labourers were not fully employed on the land.

In Continental markets English wool was much sought after, as it was considered to be the most suitable for weaving fine cloth. The wool merchants of East Anglia, busily fulfilling the increased demand for their goods, were becoming exceedingly prosperous, to such an extent that the King, with one eye greedily on his own exchequer, now imposed still higher taxation on those who exported the raw wool.

Fig. 1

Prior Henry at once saw the opportunity to develop the cloth trade in England. And where better to put his ideas into practice than at Bocking, within his own manor, conveniently situated in the heart of East Anglian sheep farming country? One fulling mill was already operating there, and under the guidance of his monks the nucleus of a cottage industry was being developed quite successfully.

The shrewd Prior wasted no time. Forthwith he issued instructions for the thorough renovation of the old fulling mill.

He then secured from Henry de Bockynge a 'release for ever' of all claim to the mill in favour of the Convent of Christ Church.[15] The following year, 1304, he summoned to Bocking a group of skilled Flemish craftsmen in order that the local people might be taught the art of weaving a finer type of cloth.

From that day Bocking never looked back. In the wake of the Flemish weavers came people from neighbouring districts ready to settle in the town and to learn the trade. Other fulling mills were established. Within a short time considerable business was being carried on, processing the wool, weaving and selling cloth. Everyone connected with the trade, whether a fuller, teazler, dyer or weaver, belonged to a craft guild which protected his interests as well as the rights of master and apprentice. There is said to have been a Guild Hall in Church Street, near the present *King William* inn.

The medieval town was now a hive of activity and its houses soon extended beyond the little Church Street community. Some of the newcomers, or 'clothiers' as the manufacturers of woollen cloth came to be called, settled along that part of the old Roman road from Braintree which was known as Bradford Street, taking its name from the broad ford across the Blackwater river. Here they enjoyed the dual advantage of proximity to the fulling mills and a position on the main trade thoroughfare between London and the east coast ports. In time, as these clothiers grew rich, they built themselves fine timbered dwellings along Bradford Street. Unfortunately the few clothiers' houses which still stand today are in a poor state of repair, but one, now called 'Tudor House', has been restored and opened in 1974 as a local museum. Carpenters' marks may be seen on some of the timbers, and it is believed that these houses were 'prefabricated' in barns or workshops and assembled on the site, local clay being mixed with straw and plastered onto a framework of cleft oak splines and wattle. Many of the Bocking clothiers handsomely endowed the parish church, and in St. Mary's there exist several interesting memorials to the generosity of these merchants.

The history of the local cloth trade merits a book of its own and will be sketched in here merely as a background to the story of the Deanery. In many ways the two are inseparable, for without the immense wealth acquired by town and Church through this trade there might never have been an elegant Deanery house, nor such illustrious deans as those who held office there during its heyday. Without the worthy clothiers and their families who formed the backbone of the parish for hundreds of years there would be no tale to tell.

The Parish Church

During the Middle Ages it was customary among the thriving wool towns of East Anglia for local squires and wealthy citizens to spend vast sums of money on enlarging and beautifying their local church. In some cases they did so out of all proportion to the size of the congregation. This was not true at Bocking, where the growth in population more than justified the improvements. At Bocking, too, the monks could count on the support of their Archbishop and were fortunate in securing other generous benefactors, all of whom are suitably commemorated in the church.

The inspiration behind the renovations emanated from William Courtenay soon after his appointment as Archbishop of Canterbury in 1381. Courtenay, of whom it was said that he 'upheld the papal authority in England, although not to the injury of the English Church', had previously been Bishop of London, and he had a country manor house on Chapel Hill, at Braintree. A son of the Earl of Devon and grandson of Edward I, he was appointed Lord High Chancellor of England that same year, and in 1382 officiated at the marriage of Richard II to Anne of Bohemia. High rank does not seem to have interfered with his personal interest in Bocking, however, for in addition to planning the new church he made himself financially responsible for much of the fabric in it. He also sanctioned the use of the Courtenay family crest on the first Deanery seal, which was designed during the Archbishopric and probably at his instigation. This early seal, now extinct—it was replaced by the present design in 1596—is said to have portrayed the Madonna and Child in a tabernacle, with the figure of a monk below and three shields upon one of which was represented the Courtenay dolphin.

Another early benefactor was William Doreward, the squire of Doreward's Hall, close to Bocking.[16] He founded a chantry at Bocking in 1362 and established a family tradition of endowing the church which was continued through three generations.

The rebuilding appears to have been undertaken in three stages: between 1385 and 1422, through the generosity of William Courtenay and the Doreward family; around 1450, when money was raised by the master clothiers of the town and supplemented by generous donations from local landowners such as the de Vere family, Earls of Oxford, and Henry Bourchier, Earl of Essex; and again in the years 1490-1520, when, in addition to the Archbishop and other wealthy patrons, several local merchants whose wills were proved at Bocking, left handsome bequests specifically for the embellishment of the church.

At the time of the first reconstruction, in 1385, north and south aisles were built on to the existing Norman church, with chapels at their eastern ends enclosed by wooden screens. The south aisle was provided by William Doreward, in accordance with the custom that those who had been granted the privilege of founding a chantry also added to the fabric of the church. Most of his family are buried in the chapel here. The earliest surviving memorials are to William's son, the eminent John Doreward, a lawyer and knight of the shire of Essex, who became Speaker of the House of Commons, and his young second wife, Isabella Baynard of Messing. Their brass figures, which for many years were hidden under the organ, have now been placed in the floor of the south aisle, but the original inscriptions are lost. It is of interest that John Doreward is here depicted in armour and not in his robes of office. In his younger days he had fought at Agincourt, and the dagger at his side and the lion at his feet are tributes to his chivalry and courage. The beautiful Isabella wears the horned head-dress and fashionable costume of the period, richly trimmed with fur.

In 1397 the same John Doreward founded a second chantry in the north aisle chapel and purchased a small plot of land from the monks of Christ Church in order to endow this and the earlier chantries in perpetuity. The reasons behind his action are clearly stated in the foundation charter still preserved at Canterbury:

Because in these days divine worship is diminished rather than increased, the souls of the deceased are more quickly forgotten as the devotions of the living are withdrawn from the churches to an unwonted extent.[17]

Here we detect the influence of Archbishop Courtenay, a bitter opponent of Wycliffe and the Lollard movement which was then beginning to gain momentum, decrying the wealth and ritual of the English Church.

On the land he purchased (now part of the churchyard), Doreward built a house for the chantry priest, whose duties were most strictly defined. He was not to absent himself from the house for more than 30 days in the year, and then only for proper cause, such as to visit friends, to obtain medicine, to join a pilgrimage or to defend the rights of the chantry. He was to hold no other benefice and to receive no stipend from another source, nor was he to be the parish priest in Bocking church or elsewhere. On Sundays and the greater festivals he was to assist in the church, wearing his surplice. Under pain of dismissal he was forbidden to frequent taverns or to consort with disreputable or suspicious persons. He was to hand over all oblations and money offerings to the Rector of Bocking.

No doubt the worthy benefactor was concerned that the priest might have too much time on his hands, but from the growth of the parish at this period it is more than likely that he was kept fully occupied. It is on record that by the year 1548 no less than two priests were employed at Bocking, assisting the Dean with the duties of his parish and teaching the local children to read and write in the Chapel of St. Nicholas.

In 1415 work began on a west tower of noble proportions. It is believed that John Doreward, then at the height of his fame, put up the money for the building of this tower, for work on it appears to have been suspended halfway through, probably in 1422, the date of his death. The two lower stages are faced with freestone, an expensive material which in those days had to be brought some distance by horse-drawn transport or even on the back of mules, and springers and vaults in the ringers' loft suggest an original intention to finish off the tower with a fine vaulted roof of stone. Years later it was completed in flint rubble, to a lesser height, giving the tower its present somewhat squat appearance. The arms of the donor and his wife were painted on shields hung above the door, while niches flanking the entrance to the south porch then contained the figures of the Blessed Virgin, St. Nicholas, St. Katherine, and St. Anne, so that the saints might bless the comings and goings of the congregation. These have been replaced by modern figures, while on the architraves of the door are painted carvings of the heads of Henry III and his wife, Eleanor of Provence.

The Doreward family tradition was carried on by John, son of the Speaker, who built, in about 1440, on land belonging to his estate, the *Maison de Dieu,* which he endowed to house seven poor people of the parish. The present Almshouses were rebuilt in 1869 on the same site.

More extensive work was carried out in the years following 1450. The old Norman arches of the nave were taken down and rebuilt, and taller Gothic windows inserted in both aisles. On one of the window-stops here two of the donors are commemorated. The stone carving of mullet and rose, representing the rowel of a knightly spur and the red rose of Lancaster, is that of John de Vere, 12th Earl of Oxford, who lived at Castle Hedingham. A staunch Lancastrian, he was beheaded in 1462 during the Wars of the Roses. Below this there are the knot and water-bouget (a medieval water-carrier made of skin), badges of Henry, Viscount Bourchier of Stanstead Hall, Halstead, treasurer to King Edward IV and created Earl of Essex in 1461. The original Courtenay doors were not touched, and although in recent years the outer stonework has had to be restored, their inner arches remain intact.

It was during the period 1490 to 1520 that the church was rebuilt largely in its present form. The chancel, the two chapels and the chancel arch were renewed; the nave was heightened and upper windows inserted to make a clear-storey, so letting more light into the interior. The mitre and arms of the See of Canterbury carved in the spandrels over the nave indicate that Archbishop Warham, who crowned Henry VIII in 1509 and was the bitter rival of Cardinal Wolsey, became one of St. Mary's benefactors at this time. There is also a mullet honouring John de Vere, 13th Earl of Oxford, who in 1485 commanded the archers at the battle of Bosworth Field which ended the Wars of the Roses and placed the first Tudor king on the English throne. These emblems appear again on the bosses of the north and south aisles, together with a leopard's head, the crest of the Fitch family of Lyons Hall nearby. The original stained glass windows of the south aisle bore the arms of the Priory of Christ Church, Canterbury—the familiar silver cross on a blue field with the Greek *XI* for Christ.

In 1503 William Claryon, a local clothier, directed in his will that his house and lands were to be sold 'and the money therof takyn to bē disposed to the welth of the church of Bokkyng for a Rhode lofte to be made there'. His example was followed by William Nobyll of Bocking, who in 1517 left £20 'to the Gyldying of Le Roodelofte' and by John Maye who gave a similar sum for the same purpose. Both of these were substantial bequests, taking into account the value of money in the 16th century. A handsome rood-loft was eventually constructed over the chancel-screen, with access from stairs contained in the turret outside the north aisle. It was not to remain there very long, however, for rood-lofts were abolished by King Edward VI.

When the masonry work was finished, a splendid timber roof was added to the church, to replace the Norman thatch. These old timbers were to last for nearly 400 years, until they were reinforced with steel joists after the roof nearly collapsed at Matins one Sunday in 1896. Next, the upper stages of the tower were completed and a south porch built on. Apart from the clock-bell which was added later, the church then must have looked much as it does today, with its solid outer walls of flint rubble and limestone. A massive wall was built round the churchyard, using similar flint rubble with moulded stone copings. About a century later this wall was reinforced with brick and the gateway that once led to the chantry priest's house was filled in, there being no longer any use for it after all chantries were dissolved by order of Edward VI in 1547. Part of the original wall still stands on the south and west sides of the churchyard; because it was designed to protect the church against invaders and had to be repaired by successive generations with whatever material was available at the time, it contains some Roman tiles, some flint and 'rubble and some early brick, and two of the several gun-rests that once existed may still be seen on the west side. The north wall was rebuilt in brick during the 17th century.

Great must have been the pride and rejoicing in Bocking when the reconstruction was complete in about 1520. The work had taken so many years that the church was now part Gothic, part Perpendicular in style. Dedicated to St. Mary the Virgin and built on rising ground on the north bank of the river, it was visible *for miles around, a splendid monument to the glory of God. Joyfully, the church bells rang out in celebration, and people came from the surrounding hamlets to look and to admire. The original bells have long since disappeared: of the present peal the earliest date from the end of the 17th century, as we shall see later.

There had been a church at Bocking for nearly 600 years. And in accordance with the terms of the old charter, there daily prayers had been offered to God for the repose of the souls of its two Saxon benefactors by the Canterbury monks. Now the wind of change was beginning to blow. Within 20 years the monks would vanish from the scene, dispossessed of their lands and their accumulated wealth by order of the King.

Many changes were to follow in the wake of the Dissolution which would affect the lives of English people— clergy and layman, landowner and peasant. None of them could have been foreseen by anyone in Bocking that day in 1520. Least of all would Thomas Wodyngton, the Rector, as he made his way from the church across the wooden bridge and along the well-trodden path towards the rectory, have suspected the future that lay ahead for his modest timber-framed dwelling built on glebe land to the south-west of St. Mary's: the official residence of the future Deans of Bocking, a Deanery across whose threshold many eminent persons—and among them at least one Royal guest—would set foot in years to come? Such thoughts would surely not have entered the priest's head as he approached the house.

III

PRIEST'S HOUSE TO DEANERY

'One hide . . . I give to the church, for the priest who serves God there.'

By these words, written in his will, Aetheric secured for all time a considerable freeholding, or glebe, for the Bocking parish priest. Such provision was fundamental to the parochial system then developing in England. No bishop would agree to consecrate a church unless he were satisfied that the landowner on whose estate it stood had set aside an adequate portion of land to house and support the priest.

During Aetheric's lifetime the priest was probably housed in a simple hut-like dwelling close to the church. But when the monks of Christ Church took possession of Bocking manor in 1006, they were obliged under the terms of the charter to allocate one hide of land to the priest. Obviously it was to their advantage to hold on to the land immediately surrounding the manor house, and so they relinquished a few acres of ground on the opposite bank of the river. On this glebeland, now Deanery Hill, the priest built a simple house, raised a few cattle and pigs and grew what crops he could to make a living. The Rector of Bocking has dwelt there since that time.

The average English country parson had a rather thin existence throughout the 11th and 12th centuries. Under the patronage of the lord of the manor, a rector had customarily been entitled to certain tithes on the lands and crops of the parish, in return for which he was responsible for the upkeep of the chancel of the church and for the good repair of his own dwelling. But when the religious houses took over the lands, as at Bocking, they also appropriated the incumbent's tithes. This meant that although the monks were now liable for the maintenance of the church, the rector was deprived of all income other than that he could raise from the produce of his glebe. It is not surprising that many clerics tried to hold down a number of appointments simultaneously, or that their houses fell into disrepair.

During the later Middle Ages the bishops and secular authorities did much to improve the lot of the parish priest, and by the end of the 14th century he usually had been granted security of tenure and an adequate income. This covered his basic food, clothing and household expenses; but it must be remembered that his standard of living was low, for the average priest of the period was drawn from the peasant class and was both made to feel, and kept, inferior to the monks, socially and scholastically.

We have already seen that at Bocking the parson was better off than many others. Morant, in his *History of Essex,* writes of its 'valuable rectory' with a glebe of 108 acres. Out of the income this yielded, the Dean must have been in a position to provide a decent living and a good house for the incumbent.

The northern wing of the Old Deanery was once the priest's house. If, with a little imagination, we strip away the later additions and the landscaped gardens, we can visualise the rectangular timber-framed hall as it was then, nestling comfortably alongside the tithe barn and other outbuildings of the glebe farm.

It is not of course the earliest priest's house built on the site. Between the 11th and 13th centuries there must have been several, for in those days a house was not constructed to last. Quite apart from the fact that the priest often had insufficient means to keep his property in a good state of repair, and so let it go derelict, leaving his successor to build a new one, there were the constant hazards of fire and plunder which might wreck the wooden structure at any time.

The dating of an old property is extremely hazardous. In the absence of records there is rarely anything to go on beyond a few fragments of the original foundations, some roof-timbers or some wattle and daub. Subsequent restoration and refenestration has to be taken into account, and also that in rural districts houses often continued to be built in an earlier style than was fashionable in the towns, sometimes for a century of more. Where original timbers have been re-used in new positions at a later date, it becomes even more difficult to make any accurate assessment.

The floor-joists and rafters here indicate that the oldest part of the Deanery was probably built in about the year 1300.

In the early Middle Ages it was customary for man and beast to live under one roof, and the Bocking priest's house may have been divided into two parts, one of which accommodated his horse and livestock. Excavations beneath the floor in one corner of the house revealed a drain that probably served the stabling area—it appears to have been linked to an outside duct running through what is now the rose garden. The priest who first lived here ate and slept with the members of his household in the other half of the house, at very close quarters. The stench must have been terrible and only partially relieved by cooking smells or smoke from the wood fire, not all of which could escape through the slits in the roof. Refinements such as chimneys and glazed windows were not usual in small houses of this type until late Tudor or Jacobean times.

Later, when separate stabling quarters were built, the partition was knocked down and the house took the form of one oblong hall. It probably had a raised dais at one end, with a long wooden table and a chair for the master of the house, and at the far end a wooden screen behind which were the kitchen and buttery. In the middle of one wall there would have been a rough stone hearth.

There was no upper storey in the medieval house. From the hall you could look right up to the rafters supporting the roof. One of the original rafters, heavily coated with soot, may still be seen in the attics, but in a new position.

As to how many people were accommodated in the house in the Middle Ages we can only guess. Even the poorest parish priest employed a boy to clean and cook, and to groom his horse. The Bocking rector may have had two or three servants. From time to time he probably housed the chaplain or chantry priests while they built dwellings of their own, since they were well endowed for this purpose by their benefactors. There would also have been the occasional pilgrim or traveller, although so long as the monks ran their guest house by the church and the St. James hospice it is unlikely that there were many such demands on the rector—except perhaps when the Archbishop came on a visitation accompanied by his customary retinue of some 50 men.

By modern standards the interior of the priest's house would be considered bare. Most of the furnishings, such as they were—perhaps a table and chair, some stools and benches, several straw pallets and one or two tapestry wall hangings—were part of the benefice, and the incumbent had few personal belongings beyond his cooking utensils, pewter cups and dishes, some linen and rough blankets or rugs for his bed.

In those days there was no lady of the house, for priests were bound by a rule of celibacy which remained in force until the 16th century. There are said to have been many in England who kept unofficial 'wives', and perhaps those in the more remote parishes may have remained undetected. At Bocking, under the watchful eye and proximity of the Canterbury monks, the priest could scarcely have failed to observe the law.

It was not yet customary for the Rector of Bocking automatically to be collated to the office of dean, although as early as the late 14th century two incumbents, Edmund de Bockingham and Thomas Grocer, had in turn served in both capacities. With the rapid growth of Bocking and the other parishes of the Peculiar at this period, it must have seemed increasingly desirable to have a resident dean. This need may well have been in the mind of the benefactor who financed the building of a solar wing on to the priest's house in the early Tudor period, probably at about the same time as the first major reconstruction of the church was undertaken.

The real incentive to appoint a dean who would live in Bocking did not arise, however, until after the Dissolution, when Bocking Hall no longer belonged to the Church.

The Tudor Rebuilding

The work of converting a simple priest's house into one suitable for a dean may have been carried out in several stages. It was probably completed before 1565, the year in which the first dean known to have taken up residence at Bocking was appointed.

The basic shape of the house—an oblong hall with a service
wing at one end—was not altered. A first floor was built
above it on the 'H' plan then popular both in Essex and other
parts of the country. In the roof above the old service wing a
'priest's hole' has been discovered and also a queen-post which
is believed to date from the 12th or 13th century. Such
posts were much used in the roof-work of Essex churches at
that date.

The new solar wing was left open to the rafters, and here
too, now enclosed in the attic, there are fine examples of the
old builder's craft in the three-bay roof: crown-posts and a
collar-purlin. The upper chamber of this wing must have been
a magnificent room, with the woodwork painted in blue,
terracotta and black and a fresco some two feet deep in a
design of roses and green briars running round all four walls.
Fragments of this fresco and part of a gilded mural were
uncovered during restoration work a few years ago, and a small
section has been preserved under glass.

Other refinements added to the house at this time include
the central chimney-stack and several mullioned windows. Two
of these windows, facing south-west, in the ground floor room
(once the drawing room) have oak mullions of this period; for
many years they were buried under plaster, with the result
that they are in a remarkably fine state of preservation. Two
similar windows in the north-west wall of the room formerly
used as the study, looking onto the present terrace, have been
found by the restorers, and also a medieval doorway leading
into the study from the drawing room.

When the rebuilding was finished and the steeply-gabled
façade had been plastered—it must be remembered that the
front of the house faced what is now the terrace and the
lawn—Bocking Rectory (for it was not yet officially the
Deanery) must have resembled a prosperous manor house.
Around it, now of sizeable proportions, were various outbuildings: the tithe barn, a granary, stables, cowsheds and
piggeries, and probably also a brew-house and bake-house.
There were no formal gardens then, for every acre of the glebe
was of necessity put to good use either as pastureland, cornfield
or orchard. If the Rector happened to be a keen agriculturist
as well as a cleric (and inevitably some were better than others)

the property was not only well-kept but brought in a good income.

Dissolution of the Monasteries

When Henry VIII dispossessed the religious houses in 1539, seizing the manor of Bocking, among many others, for the Crown, all that remained to the See of Canterbury were the parish church and the rectory glebe, a total of just over 100 acres. The monks disappeared from the manor house, and with them a way of life that had existed for 600 years.

One effect of the Dissolution was that the parish priest, who had previously served his Dean under the daily supervision of the monks, now found himself directly responsible to the Dean, as were the rectors of Hadleigh and the other parishes within the Peculiar. Since the Dean of Bocking did not at that time permanently reside there, it was imperative that the rectors of the Peculiar should be men of some status and learning. Soon it became customary for the rectors to take up residence in their parish—although this did not prevent many of them managing to hold lucrative appointments elsewhere and leaving the administration of their parishes to the chaplain and chantry priests or, after the Dissolution of the Chantries in 1547, to curates whom they appointed specifically to assist them in their duties. Bocking, so the historian Morant has recorded, 'was then a market town and had in it to the number of 800 of houseling people'.[18]

From this time on the Archbishops of Canterbury have followed the practice of conferring the title of Dean upon the Rector of Bocking. Today, the incumbent receives his commission from the archbishop as Dean of Bocking usually within a few weeks of his institution as Rector.

The second half of the 16th century was most eventful in the history of Bocking. Within months of seizing the manor, Henry VIII sold it to Roger Wentworth of Felsted (son of Sir Roger Wentworth of Codham Hall) for the sum of £875 11s. 3d. The King also disposed of the chantry lands: the Stafford endowment, then valued at £6 17s. 8d. was granted to Edward Bury, and the Doreward lands, worth £8 0s. 5d. annually, were divided between Anthony Aucher and Henry Polsted.[18a]

The new lord of the manor, who came to live at Bocking Hall, lost no time in proving himself a benefactor to the church. His clock-bell, which originally hung in a cupola on top of the tower, bears two medallions; both are now worn so smooth as to be unrecognisable, but one is said to be a full-length knight in armour, popularly supposed to be the bell's donor, Roger Wentworth, and the other, a bearded head in profile wearing a Tudor plumed cap, King Henry VIII. The bell has always been known as 'Bell Richard' because of its dedication to Richard of Chichester, the saint of husbandry, a reminder that in spite of its rapidly-increasing textile industry, 16th-century Bocking still had many acres under the plough. the Latin inscription, 'NOMEN SI QUERIS QUIUS VOCOR IPSE RICARDUS' is translated as 'If you ask the name by which I am called, it is Richard'. It is believed that the bell was cast in 1540 by the well-known Flemish founder, Johannes Tonne, who had migrated first to Sussex and then to Essex in about 1536. Its clockworks have been restored twice, but the original bell is chiming still.

The Wentworth family are buried in the north aisle of the chancel, which once contained their handsome brass effigies and an inscription to the memory of the first private owners of Bocking Hall:

> Of your charity pray for the souls of Roger Wentworth Esquire, Mary, Alice and Anne his wifes; by the said Alice he had issued 2 sonnes and one daughter. Wch Roger dyed 24 day of Febr. 1556 whose soul Jesu pardon.

Nonconformists and Puritans

A storm was now brewing in the Church. Henry VIII had taken the first steps towards the Reformation by breaking with Rome in 1534 and by declaring himself 'supreme Head of the English Church'. There followed a period of swift Protestant advance during the reign of Henry's son, the young Edward VI, reversed by a return to Catholicism under Mary. It was a time of great bitterness and unrest, when many were burned at the stake or forced into exile for their faith. Queen Elizabeth, on her accession in 1558, tried to steer a middle course, but by this time the Puritan movement, inspired by the doctrines of the great Continental reformers, Luther and Calvin, and the Scotsman, John Knox, were fast establishing a stronghold throughout the country.

In Bocking there was much interest in the new ideas. In January 1551 the Council thought fit to enquire into a meeting of some 60 persons that had been held 'at the house of one Upcharde, in Bocking, apparently an inn' where they had discussed 'thinges of the Scripture, speciallie wheather it were necessarie to stande or kneele barehedde or covered at prayer; which at length was concluded in ceremonie not to be materiall, but the hartes before God was it that imported and no thing els.'[19]

A few years later, four laymen from Bocking were among a group of six who were sent up to London from Essex on charges of heresy, to be imprisoned in the Marshalsea.

John Nowell, who was appointed Dean of Bocking in 1556, was one who held strong Puritan views. He and his curate, a man by the name of Holland, became involved in a fierce dispute with the Rector of Stisted in 1564. Richard Kitchen, on presentation to that rectory, had apparently been enjoined by Archbishop Parker to follow the rules of the Church however persuaded by others of the contrary. Nowell, as Dean of the Peculiar, objected to Kitchen's ministering in his surplice and facing east, and particularly to his perambulating the parish with his parishioners during Rogation week, in accordance with ancient custom, to say 'certain offices in certain places'.

On the following Sunday, from Stisted pulpit, Holland denounced Kitchen for this practice, whereupon the enraged Rector wrote direct to the Archbishop informing him of the gross irregularities of the Puritan clergy in the district. Some of them, he said, 'conferred baptisms in basins, some in dishes, rejecting the use of the font . . . some held there must be seven godfathers; some would either that every father should christen his own child, or at least admit him to be chief godfather; some took down the font and painted a great bowl and caused to be written on the outside "Baptisme" . . . some taught that women might not pray in Rogation week'. As an example of those who 'detested the surplice in ministration' he alleged that at Bocking it had been 'laid-a-water' by Holland the curate there for many a day. This information, together with other similar allegations, was laid before the Queen, who ordered the Archbishop to see to the suppression of 'such obvious Nonformity'. Her command had little effect, however, for without the support of Parliament Matthew Parker was powerless to stem the rise of Puritanism.[20]

The following year, for reasons we do not know for certain— although it was rumoured that he was carrying out the personal wishes of the Queen—Parker collated to the Deanery of Bocking a young man who had seen rapid advancement in the Church and was an erudite scholar of extreme Puritan sympathies.

Thus, in the year 1565, Dr. James Calfhill arrived in Bocking to take up residence in the house on the hill once occupied by a humble parish priest, now officially designated as 'The Deanery'.

IV

SCHOLAR DEANS AND BOCKONIANS

James Calfhill

The new Dean was about 35 years of age when he came to Bocking. There are two different theories as to his family origin: one that he was a native of Edinburgh, the other that he was a Shropshire man. His name is sometimes recorded as 'Calfield', but in Essex he has always been known as Dean Calfhill. By all accounts he was something of a firebrand, a strong personality who must have made considerable impact on the parish.

He had been educated at Eton during the headmastership of the celebrated playwright Nicholas Udall, who, incidentally, was at the time also vicar of Braintree, paying a curate to discharge his duties there in his absence. Although Udall's *Ralph Roister Doister*, the earliest known English comedy, was not written until later, the boys at Eton were encouraged to act in other dramatic productions, and, presumably influenced by Udall, Calfhill himself later became a noted writer, chiefly of comic Latin verse. He also wrote a Latin tragedy which was performed before the Queen when she visited Oxford in 1566, but, according to the historian who recorded the event, although 'it had applause, and he received her thanks . . . it took not half so well as the comedy . . .'.[21]

From Eton Calfhill went to King's College, Cambridge, but three years later he enrolled as a student at the new foundation of Christ Church at Oxford, where he took his B.A. in 1549. Having taken his M.A. in 1522, he remained in Oxford for several years, probably filling some post at the University. He was very much influenced by the Reformation doctrines, and there is little doubt that he would have entered Holy Orders sooner had it not been for the death of Edward VI the following year.

To have become a member of the clergy under the Catholic regime of Mary would have gone against his inner conscience. It is said that the young scholar was so incensed by some Latin verses written by Dr. John White, then Bishop of Lincoln, to honour the marriage of the Queen to Philip II of Spain in 1554, that he promptly composed—and published—some fiery lines in reply. How he managed to escape punishment for this daring act, is not known.

Within two months of the accession of Elizabeth, Calfhill became a deacon, and in June 1560 he took priest's orders. The following summer, two days after his ordination, he was made a Canon of Christ Church, Oxford. Other promotions followed rapidly, and he acquired a reputation as 'an elegant scholar, a forcible preacher and a staunch Calvinist'.[22] He was especially praised by a friend of John Foxe for a sermon delivered at St. Paul's Cross in January 1560/1 in which he eloquently bewailed the bondage of Oxford to the 'papistical yoke'. Of another sermon a contemporary wrote' 'The promising Christ Church man, Calfhill, preached with an excellent tongue and rhetorical tale which ravished the minds of his hearers'.[23]

Rector of St. Andrew Wardrobe in London in 1562, and Prebendary of St. Paul's Cathedral later the same year, Calfhill took his degree of Doctor of Divinity in May 1565 and was immediately collated to the Deanery of Bocking. Two months later he was appointed Archdeacon of Colchester.

Such rapid preferment combined with extreme Puritanical views did not make for much popularity with the clergy over whom he had jurisdiction. He is said to have introduced new charges every year in his visitation and to have encouraged irregularities. Many complaints reached Archbishop Parker concerning his administration. One concerned a sermon preached before the Queen, when it was alleged that 'the vigorous Calfhill distinguished himself to the disgust of the temperate Haddon by a sermon full of contention. It was a downright challenge . . . it was most offensive. The Queen's presence demands more decency than that. No one has ever given less satisfaction in that capacity. Everyone was annoyed; the more so because he is a master of the pulpit and a fine orator. Vanity is the plague of genius.'[24]

Either the Queen was less disturbed than the courtiers who were present on that occasion, or she had a shorter memory, for although Robert Cecil subsequently refused Calfhill the Provostship of King's College, Cambridge, for which he applied in 1569, a greater honour was yet to come his way. In June 1570, Elizabeth nominated him to the Bishopric of Worcester. He was then 40 years old.

By this time Dean Calfhill had spent five years at Bocking. Regrettably there are no records which throw light upon his life at the Deanery. He is said to have had a wife, which may be correct, for the Queen, while not exactly encouraging her clergy to marry, did not forbid their marriage and frequently promoted married priests to high positions in the Church.

Tudor men and women knew how to live. Now that there was a mistress in the house, the interior of the Deanery must have been both attractively furnished and comfortable. The floor of the original hall was probably boarded over, and local craftsmen would have been employed to panel some of the rooms, to build closets and internal doors and to mould the ceilings. In winter a huge fire would have blazed in the wide hearth, now provided with a proper chimney. Gay silken cushions, wall hangings and perhaps a family portrait or two would be prominently displayed in the main room. In the solar there would have been a spinning wheel, and on the first floor a canopy bed. Pewter and silver ornaments added decoration, and the Dean must also have owned a number of beautifully-bound books. In front of the house, where the terrace now is, there may have been a small garden.

Calfhill was almost certainly a man of means. But even if he had had to depend on the rectorial tithes for his living, the income these provided would have been ample to keep him and his wife in the grand manner. Less fortunate members of the clergy in other parts of England, faced with the sudden debasement of coinage and the rise in living costs that had resulted from the Dissolution, found themselves in desperate straits. Not so at Bocking, where the cloth trade was booming, and where wool and corn were fetching excellent prices. The learned Doctor probably built a farmhouse and put in a bailiff to run the glebe farm. The domestic quarters would also have been enlarged at this time to accommodate more servants.

Then, in the summer of 1570, shortly before he was due to be consecrated as Bishop of Worcester, the Dean fell fatally ill. He died at the Deanery and was buried in the parish church. No memorial has survived, and the Bocking burial register contains one simple entry:

'1570. Doctor Jacobus Calfhill sepultus est. Aug. 22.'

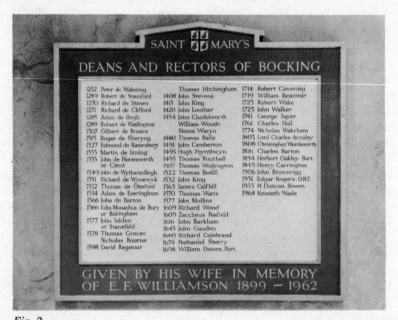

Fig. 2

Twin Deans

The next Dean was Thomas Watts, about whom little is known except that he was also Archdeacon of Middlesex and a man of considerable learning. By a codicil to his will dated 24 May 1577,[25] he bequeathed to the library of Pembroke Hall, Cambridge, certain books from his study in London and 'also all such other books at my house at Bocking as my good Lord Archbishop of Canterbury shall think meet for the library'. Watts held the appointment at Bocking from 1570 until his death in 1577 and had the distinction of being the first of the 'Twin Deans'—although this title was not thought of until much later.

It was in November 1572 that Archbishop Parker established the precedent by appointing the Rector of Hadleigh as a joint Dean of Bocking. What prompted him in this, we do not know, but it may have been that the incumbent of Hadleigh at this time was a most eminent scholar, Dr. John Still, who was later to be Master, first of St. John's and then of Trinity College, Cambridge, and eventually Bishop of Bath and Wells. It was also possible that he intended one Dean to look after the Peculiar parishes in Essex and the other those in Suffolk.

For the next few years it is unlikely that any of the deans or rectors of Bocking spent much time at the Deanery. They were nearly all wealthy, learned men who could well afford to pay one or more curates to take care of their parochial duties. This is not to say that they did not visit Bocking regularly: they must have done so in order to hold the Deanery courts and to supervise the clergy under their control. But their main duties lay elsewhere.

John Mullins, or Molyns, for instance, who became Rector of Bocking in 1577 on the death of Watts and was commissioned as Dean jointly with John Still in 1583, was at the same time a Canon of St. Paul's Cathedral and an Archdeacon of London. A Fellow of Magdalen College, Oxford, he died in June 1591, leaving £200 to purchase lands for the endowment of two scholars at that College. He is buried in the north aisle of St. Paul's beneath a fine memorial slab.

Of Richard Wood and Zaccheus Pasfield, who at the turn of the century held office as deans of Bocking together with George Meriton, Rector of Hadleigh, we know even less.

An interesting document survives from the time of John Mullins, but, unfortunately, it is so badly damaged that parts of it are illegible. Dated 1590, it is an exemplification of the extent of the manor made by the Dean and Chapter of Canterbury at Mullins's special request.[26] The text is in Latin. A complete breakdown of the lands is given, down to the value of each acre per annum. Bockinge Park is said to contain an estimated 'hundred handspans' of wood and underwood, with herbage worth 12 pence per annum and pannage (pasture-land for swine) worth 10 shillings per annum. There is 'arable land in the demesne in various fields 110 acres more or less and each acre is worth 6 pence per annum'. Of this arable land, 'an acre can suitably be sowed with two and a half bushells of corn . . . and two and a half bushells of oats full measure, two and a half bushells of peas, three bushells . . .[the Latin is illegible here] and four bushells of barley. And a plough can usually plough an acre a day . . . yoke of six horses and two oxen'. The meadowland is worth 56 shillings per year, 30 acres of pasture with tracks leading to it suitable for oxen and horses worth 12 pence per acre per annum, and 24 acres of pasture for cows 'next to land of the lord in various places, some of it let, four shillings'.

Another charter (undated) which follows immediately after the one previously quoted concerns a dispute that evidently had arisen between the Rector and one of his parishioners concerning a right of way. A search having been made at Canterbury, the charter confirms that a record has been found of 'the Recognition of men of Bockinge of the way to the meadow of the rector of Bockinge'. The scribe dutifully copied out the old text which, from its style and content, appears to date from the 11th or 12th century. We read that Walter de Bockinge, Stephen son of Roger, Martin the clerk, Roger de Bronketr' and 12 others whose names are given all testified that the Rector 'should have and has been accustomed to have his way to his meadow, which belongs to Bocking church, through the meadows of Nicholas Pruet, to cart his hay and not otherwise unless by permission'.[27]

'Good and Trewe Clothe'

By the mid-16th century Bocking was fast making a reputation for the excellent woollen cloth that was woven in the town. No less than three fulling mills were working in 1556. It was a period in which many cloth merchants made vast fortunes and turned themselves into 'landed' gentlemen. Described in an Act of Parliament passed during the reign of Queen Elizabeth as a 'fayre large Towne . . . inhabited of a long time with Clothe makers which have made and dayle do make good and trewe clothe', the town had almost doubled its working population in the space of 30 years, reaching a total of 1,500 by the year 1575. It was to go on increasing for another 50 years. Of all the Essex weaving towns Bocking was second in importance only to Colchester.

The extent of the local cloth trade at this period must not be judged by population, however, for Bocking clothiers employed hundreds of weavers and spinners from the surrounding hamlets. It has been said that these clothiers grew rich while their workers starved. Certainly the wages they paid—sixpence a day—were insufficient to keep a family without supplementary produce from the land. This was the crux of the problem. For the spinning and weaving industry which had begun as a profitable spare-time occupation for the country folk now required regular workers, and it was these unsuspecting people who came to settle in the town who found it difficult to make ends meet. Agricultural wages had always been considered as a supplement to what the labourer could produce from his own plot of ground, and the local justices who were responsible for fixing wages still thought in terms of the wage earner having his strip of land. The new town dwellers had no such resources. Complaints to the Essex Quarter Sessions were frequent, and in April 1599 the Court ordered 'the matter in variance between the clothiers and weavers of Bocking and Braintree shall be referred to my Lord Suffragan, Francis Harvye, John Tyndall, Ralph Wyseman, Henry Maxey and Thomas Walgrave, esquires, to end and determine all controversy between them if they can, and to certify their proceedings at the next Sessions'.[28]

Bocking was famous for two types of cloth: *bay*, a coarse kind of blanket cloth or baize, and *say*, a much finer product, the earliest form of serge. Those who worked in the trade described themselves as 'bay weavers' or 'say weavers'; their employers were, in the style of the period, 'clothiers'. At the end of the 16th century the industry was still organised on a domestic system, that is to say the raw wool was bought by the clothiers and not sold until woven. Sometimes it was sold as it came from the loom, but more prosperous merchants were able to get a better price by selling the cloth dyed and finished. Quantities of the bays and says produced Bocking were sold abroad.

Inevitably there was a good deal of rivalry between the various Essex cloth towns. In 1557 an Act of Parliament referred to the counterfeiting of 'Cockshall, Bocking and Braintree cloths', and soon after 1572 the town was granted the right to use a distinctive seal on all cloth made in the town.

The Dolphin Seal

In 1596 Queen Elizabeth granted a new seal to the Deanery of Bocking. Exactly why the earlier seal of 1381 fell into disuse is not clear. It may have been connected with the fact that it did not bear the arms of Christ Church, Canterbury. Decanal seals were important ecclesiastical instruments which were appended to all official documents emanating from a particular deanery. They were seals of office, and as such did not bear the name or arms of the Dean, who may also have used his own personal seal bearing the family crest.

The new Deanery seal was pointed oval in shape and measured approximately 2¾in. by just over 1½in. Its design incorporated the plain cross of the Christ Church shield with the four Courtenay dolphins in the cantons. Above the shield there was a branch of three cinquefoil roses, slipped and leaved, and in the base a branch of two similar roses. The edge of the seal had a beaded border, around which was inscribed 'SIGILLVM - DECANI - DECANATVS - DE - BOCKING - IN - COM - ESSEX - 1596'.

It is of interest how the dolphin came to be represented on the Courtenay crest. The family was of French origin. In 1150, a Courtenay daughter married a son of Louis VI of France, Louis the Fat. The eldest son of this marriage assumed the name of Courtenay and inherited the estates; in due course he became Emperor of Constantinople. So for generations this branch of the family ruled over the Byzantine empire which, essentially maritime, had from very early times used the dolphin as its symbol. Many old Byzantine coins are stamped with a dolphin, usually head down and tail in the air, entwined round a trident.

The English Courtenays, who became the Earls of Devon, adopted the dolphin on their crest out of pride in their past connection with the great Greek Empire. It came to Bocking through William Courtenay, Archbishop of Canterbury in the 14th century.

Centuries later, in the year 1927, when the town was granted official arms, the Courtenay dolphin was again incorporated in a Bocking shield, this time along with the woolpack symbolising the cloth trade, the fleur-de-lys of the Courtauld family who built up a great commercial enterprise from small local beginnings, and the chevrons of several other prominent Bocking families. Its motto is *Consilio et Concordia*—by counsel and good fellowship.

'The Gentle Numismatist'

In December 1616 there came to the Deanery a man with a great reputation not only as a distinguished theologian but also as a scholar.

Dr. John Barkham (sometimes spelled 'Barcham') had been chaplain to two Archbishops of Canterbury, firstly to the anti-Puritan Richard Bancroft and more recently to George Abbot, a supporter of the Puritan movement. He was also a Prebendary of St. Paul's. In addition to ecclesiastical qualifications, the new Dean was an accomplished linguist and was

highly thought of in academic circles as an antiquary and
historian. He had taken great pains to assist his friend, John
Speed, the historian and cartographer, with the compilation of his
Historie of Great Britaine, which Speed had published in 1611.

John Barkham was born near Exeter, in the parish of
St. Mary-in-the-Moor, in about 1572. Educated at Exeter College
and at Corpus Christi, Cambridge, where he took his M.A. in
1594 and became a probationer Fellow in 1596, Barkham took
his Bachelor of Divinity degree in 1603 and was soon afterwards
appointed chaplain to Archbishop Bancroft. Little is known
of his family life, except that he had a wife—Anne, daughter
of Robert Rogers of Dartford, Kent—and one son. It is probable
that they accompanied him to Bocking.

The collation to Bocking was made by Archbishop Abbot,
and Dr. Barkham was to remain at the Deanery until his
death in 1642. He held his commission as Dean jointly with
the Rector of Hadleigh: initially with George Meriton and later,
from 1633 onwards, with Thomas Goad.

During the 26 years he spent at Bocking, Barkham must
have been assisted by several different curates. One of these
young men at least deserves mention. He was Nathaniel Rogers,
no relation of Mrs. Barkham, as far as is known, but the
second son of the most fanatical Puritan preacher in Essex,
'Roaring John' Rogers of Dedham, so called on account of
his exceptionally loud voice and fiery manner of preaching.
Young Nathaniel had been educated at Dedham grammar school
and at Emmanuel College, Cambridge. He was ordained in
1619, and the story goes that he once dared to preach against
his father's interpretation of the faith, in the latter's own
pulpit at Dedham, while the old man, who doted on him,
looked on.

Puritanism was widespread in Essex at this time, and during
his curacy at Bocking, which lasted from 1623 to 1628, Rogers
himself began to adopt puritan views. How the parish felt
about this, and what friction resulted between the Dean and
his curate, is not on record, but whenever Bockonians gathered
in the alehouse or families sat round the hearth on winter
evenings, sooner or later it must have crept into the
conversation. Opinions would have been sharply divided, for
the conflict between orthodox and Puritan ministers was a

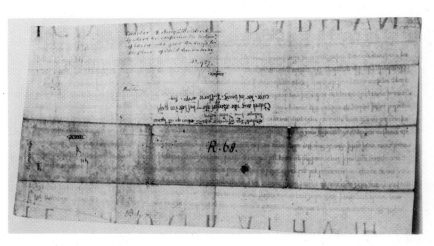

1. King Ethelred's confirmation of the Will of Aetheric of Bocking. Undated, but probably A.D. 995-999. Canterbury, *Chartae Antiquae* B.1.

2. Gift from Richard Fitzsimon to the Prior of Christ Church Canterbury of Two Deer yearly. Dated 1226. Canterbury, *Chartae Antiquae* B.255.

3. Release from Henry de Bockynge to the Prior and Convent of Christ Church for ever of all claim to a new water mill at Bockyng near Bredeford. Dated 31 Edw 1303. Canterbury, *Chartae Antiquae* B.36.

4. Licence from Edward III to the Prior and Convent of Christ Church Canterbury to empower them to hold the 20th Annual Rent, and to take and hold in perpetuity lands and tenements in Bocking and Stysted. Dated Westminster, 18 May 1355. Canterbury, *Chartae Antiquae* B.256.

5. Memorial in St. Mary's Bocking, to John Doreward (d. 1422) and his wife, Isabella Baynard of Messing.

6. *(above)* Memorial in St. Paul's to John Mullins, Dean of Bocking from 1577 to 1591. (From Dugdale's *History of St. Paul's Cathedral*, 1658.)

7. *(right)* Deanery of Bocking seal, 1596.

9. Sir William Dawes of Lyons Hall, Rector and Dean of Bocking from 1698 to 1714.

8. Dr. John Gauden, Rector and Dean of Bocking from 1642 to 1660.

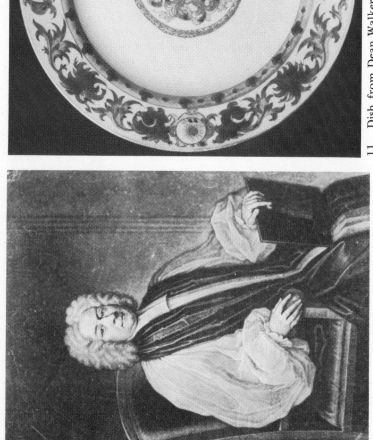

11. Dish from Dean Walker's 'Imari' style dinner service. Made at Chien Te Chen in the late K'ang Hsi period (*circa* 1720-22), it is richly decorated in Imari colours of underglaze blue and red enriched with gold and bears the arms of John Walker with, on the border, the four 'suns in splendour' family crest.

10. Dr. Robert Clavering, Rector and Dean of Bocking from 1714 to 1719.

13. Lady Charles Murray-Aynsley, who during her husband's incumbency entertained the exiled King of France, Louis XVIII, to dinner at the Deanery.

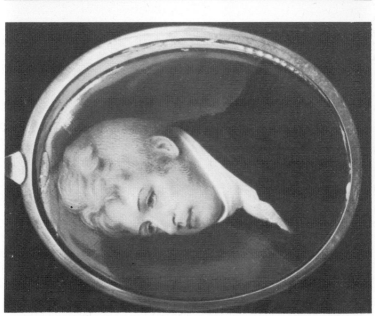

12. Lord Charles Murray-Aynsley, Rector and Dean of Bocking from 1803 to 1808.

14. Dr. Christopher Wordsworth, Rector and Dean of Bocking from 1808 to 1816.

16. Lady Oakeley (Atholl, daughter of Lord and Lady Charles Murray-Aynsley).

15. Sir Herbert Oakeley, Rector and Dean of Bocking from 1834 to 1845.

17. Dean Carrington's carriage. The same carriage was used later by Dean Brownrigg.

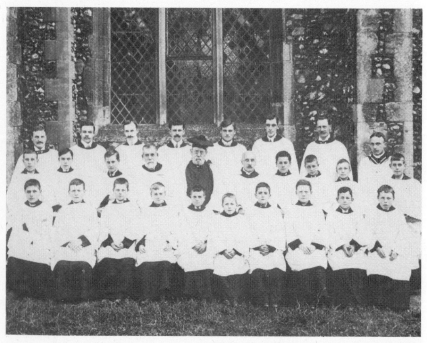

18. Dean Brownrigg, with the choir of St. Mary's, Bocking.

19. Church of St. Mary the Virgin, Bocking, from an old engraving.

20. A recent photograph of the church.

Bocking, The Deanery.

21. The Deanery, Bocking, *circa* 1900.

22. The Deanery, photographed from the same angle, 1958, showing the Victorian cement casing removed.

23. Example of fine medieval craftsmanship in the roof timbers of the Deanery.

24. Fragment of Tudor wall decoration uncovered during recent restoration work at the Deanery.

25 & 26. The Deanery, from the terrace side, before and after reconstruction, *circa* 1890 and 1958. Some of the bushes known traditionally as the 'twelve Apostles' may be seen on the left of both pictures.

bitter one and had already given rise to a number of ugly scenes in the county.

Probably Dean Barkham, a friend and loyal supporter of Archbishop Laud, tried gently to dissuade Rogers at first. By all accounts the Dean was a peaceable, gentle man. How many hours the two of them spent arguing it out, perhaps in the Deanery study, perhaps pacing up and down the garden, we can only conjecture. In any case, the older man's counsels had little effect, for Puritanism was in Roger's blood. By 1628 the situation reached the point where the Dean evidently could take no more, and he is said to have summarily dismissed the curate for not wearing a surplice when performing the burial office over an eminent parishioner. Rogers was subsequently appointed to the living of Ashington in Suffolk, but in 1636, together with his wife and six-year-old son and a band of Puritans, he emigrated to America, where he became eventually Pastor of Ipswich, Massachusetts. His son John, who graduated in theology and medicine, was to become president of Harvard in 1682.

For many years John Barkham was thought to have been the author of *A Display of Heraldrie,* the first published study on this subject, which appeared in 1610 under the name of his friend, John Guillim, later Rouge Croix Pursuivant of Arms. The story told by Sir William Dugdale that Barkham took his manuscript to Guillim and asked him to publish it in his name, as heraldry was 'too light a subject' for Barkham to touch, has now been discounted by modern historians. There is no doubt that John Barkham had an interest in heraldry, however, for his brother George was Leicester King of Arms, but it was not his pet subject.

The Dean's all-absorbing hobby was coins. He wrote a learned treatist on numismatology, which was never published, and was said to possess one of the finest collections of Greek coins in England. Barkham bequeathed his manuscript and his coins to his close friend, Archbishop Laud, who in turn presented them to the Bodleian Library at Oxford. They are now housed in the Ashmolean Museum. Twenty-nine coins of various European countries found in the tower of Corpus Christi College at Cambridge in 1648 were thought to have formed part of Barkham's original collection. Unwanted by Laud, they were probably presented by the Dean to his old college.

As a tribute to their friendship, Archbishop Laud sent to Barkham for St. Mary's Church at Bocking the very fine altar in the north chapel. It is believed that the panelling which forms a dado in the vestry was a gift of the Dean at about the same time.

At Bocking Barkham became an intimate friend of Thomas Jekyll, who then lived at Bocking Hall. Jekyll was the first of the Bocking lawyers and a well-known Essex antiquary. The Dean is said to have helped him with his historical research, and no doubt the two scholars spent many happy hours pouring over documents and coins at the Hall and Deanery. But although tribute is paid to the work of Jekyll by later Essex writers, Barkham has received no credit at all. He may have wanted it that way. He seems to have been a retiring, timid man. The late Mr. Alfred Hills, whose papers[29] contain several interesting notes about the Dean, described him as a 'gentle numismatist'.

Undoubtedly the academic Dean's happiest hours were spent pottering about his quiet study at the Deanery, sorting and cataloguing his valuable coins. In modern terminology we might call this his personal safety-valve, or bolt-hole. For there he would have felt quite remote from the troubles of 17th-century England, torn between intrigues at Court and the bitterly opposed religious factions. It is understandable that he was taken off guard, and deeply shocked, by the ugly demonstration against his friend the Archbishop that took place at Bocking in the summer of 1640.

After the accession of Charles I in 1625, the anti-Calvinist William Laud lost no time in vigorously trying to restore 'decency and uniformity' within the Church. Appointed Archbishop of Canterbury in 1633, he decreed the communion table to be of far greater importance than the pulpit, and ordered that all communion tables were to be placed at the east end of the church and enclosed by rails. Supported by the King, he next tried to force the Anglican prayer book on the Scots in place of the liturgy of John Knox. He succeeded only in driving the Scots to rebellion. The two 'Bishops' Wars' which followed were very unpopular and led to much rowdyism and disorder among English soldiers ordered against their will to fight the invading Scottish army.

One day in July 1640 there arrived at Bocking a company of soldiers who were being marched northwards against the Scots, together with their captain, a man by the name of Rowlston. They were an uncouth lot whose reputation had already reached the ears of Dr. Barkham. Misguidedly thinking that he would calm them down and win their goodwill, the Dean provided the men with a barrel of beer and 50 shillings. The soldiers immediately got drunk and became even more disorderly. They forced their way into the church and seized the communion rails, which they then burned in front of the captain's lodging. According to a contemporary account, they 'first got leave to ring the bells, then went into the chancel, declared that it was not fit that the communion table should be impounded, so they got the rails away and burnt them'. Those fine rails had been a gift to the church by Barkham, in loyalty to Laud, and it is to be hoped that the elderly Dean did not witness the sacreligious act.

The ringleader in this escapade was a certain William Bates, who was evidently bent on making trouble. When the beer was distributed and Captain Rowlston gave the toast, 'My Lord of Warwick', Bates is reported to have said, when it came to his turn to drink, 'Here's a health to my Lord of Warwick, King of Essex'. Reprimanded later for this offence, he threatened to have his senior officer's blood and was sent to the House of Correction, where, on being examined about his words, he was reported to have offered the defence 'that he had heard from someone in Huntingdonshire that Lord Warwick was King of Essex, but he spoke under the influence of drink'.[30] Sir Robert Rich, 2nd Earl of Warwick, was a fierce opponent of Laud's church policy and was backing Parliament against the King.

Perhaps the gentle Dean had grown accustomed to outbreaks of riotous behaviour during his time at Bocking. When war was declared between England and Spain in 1625, it caused one of the worst trade depressions the country had known. Suffering was particularly acute in the weaving towns of Essex,[31] for almost nine-tenths of the cloth they produced was then exported to Spain and Portugal. Hardest affected were those country people who had moved to the towns from the surrounding district and who depended exclusively on the cloth

trade for their livelihood. Unemployment grew to tremendous
proportions, and there were many cases of unruly disturbances
in the streets.

The unemployed enlisted the sympathy and support of the
Dean in their misery, and on 17 April 1629, 200 Bocking
and Braintree weavers travelled to Chelmsford to present an
appeal to the Justices of the Quarter Sessions. John Barkham's
signature headed the petition,[32] which complained of the weavers'
'extreame necessitie and disabilitie to mainteyne and relieve
themselves and theire families'. When this produced little result
beyond vague promises of help, the master weavers forwarded
a petition to the King, together with a 'declaracion concerninge
the state of the Manufacture of Wools in the countie of Essex'.
This document shows that some 33,000 cloth workers were
dependent on the production of bays and says (20,000 in
Colchester, 7,000 in Bocking, 3-4,000 in Braintree and the
rest in the nearby towns). At Bocking itself, where the trade
had been producing 400 'peeces' a week, output had fallen to
barely 40 and some of the cloth merchants had been forced to
close their businesses.

When this last petition had no effect, although it was
forwarded by the Justices of the Peace to the Privy Council,
the men of Braintree and Bocking were unable to restrain
their anger. On 22 May, 300 of them marched to Heybridge
Basin at Maldon, where they committed 'divers outrages both
in assaltinge a shippe of corne of certaine Marchants of the
north and carryinge away good quantities thereof and hurtinge
divers of the Mariners in the shipp'. They also captured and
robbed the chief merchant and stole a considerable quantity
of grain. Four of their number were caught and brought to
trial; of these, three were hanged, together with a Maldon
woman, Agnes Clarke, 'who did not only ayde from place to
place to assemble the people from Witham, Braynetree, Bockinge
etcetera but alsoe writt divers letters for that purpose wherein
she termed herself the Captaine [of the insurgents] '.[33]

Conditions did not improve. In the summer of 1642 the
troubles that had long been simmering between King and
Parliament reached their boiling point, and England was plunged
into civil war. This in turn brought further distress and hardship
to the Bocking people.

By that time, however, the Deanery had a new occupant. The 70-year-old Dr. Barkham died on 25 March 1642; he was buried in the chancel of the parish church. In his place there came certainly the most famous—and many people would say the most notorious—of all the deans of Bocking.

The Notorious Dr. Gauden

John Gauden lived at Bocking Deanery 'at a rate of a thousand a year and made the greatest figure of any clergyman in Essex, or perhaps in England at that time'.

So wrote the Reverend Dr. Anthony Walker,[34] who was Gauden's curate for several years and subsequently followed his footsteps as chaplain to the 2nd Earl of Warwick. If we consider what the mid-17th-century spending power of the pound was in terms of today, we shall have some idea of the style of living adopted by this celebrated Dean. Walker unfortunately does not disclose how Gauden's income was derived. It did not come solely from rectorial tithes, as appears from a survey of the Church lands taken at Brainteee in September 1650:

> *Bocking.* That there is in the said Parish of Bocking only one Parsonage with Cure of Souls annexed of which Dr. John Gauden is incumbent by presentation from the late Archbishop of Canterbury, Patron thereof; And that the yearly value of the Tythes there is about two hundred pounds; And there is belonging to the said Parsonage a house, garden and orchard, and also sixty Acres of glebe Land worth about thirty pounds p. ann. And that the said Dr. Gauden performeth the Cure of souls within the said parish, and is an able orthodox and godly preaching Minister, and enjoyeth the said parsonage glebe lands and tythes as aforesaid.[35]

There seems to be some discrepancy here concerning the extent of the rectory glebe, which in other records is shown as 108 or 113 acres. Possibly for the purposes of this particular survey lands leased to tenants were not included. On such lands the Dean would have received, at the time he took office, payment of fines for the renewal of leases which might have amounted to several hundred pounds. And with an income as stated amounting to £230—about five times as much as the average English parson of the day enjoyed— it is not surprising that in the mid-17th century the Deanery of Bocking was regarded as one of the most lucrative appointments in the Church. Its equivalent in terms of the 20th century, so far as income is concerned, would place it roughly between that of the Bishop of London and the Archbishop of Canterbury. Even so, it appears to have fallen far short of John Gauden's outgoings.

Taking into account not only the way he lived, but also the extensive additions and restorations Gauden made to the Deanery house during his incumbency, and the local charities he endowed, he must have been a man of considerable private wealth. Much of it was undoubtedly lavished on him by the rich patrons he cultivated. Certainly he was ambitious and shrewd: in an era of sharply-divided loyalties he somehow managed to retain the favours of both King and Parliament and to hold his lucrative Bocking appointment throughout the Civil War and the ensuing Commonwealth rule of Oliver Cromwell. He had many friends in high places, and from all accounts he did not fail to use them to his advantage. If ever there were a typical example of a man who ran with the hounds and yet hunted with the horses, Gauden was one. He probably also lived above his income: when towards the end of his life was appointed first to the bishopric of Exeter, and then to that of Worcester, he was loud in his complaints as to the 'poverty' of both Sees. And after his death, his widow did her best to get some remission of duty on the estate. There can be no doubt that their 'grand' years at Bocking had given them a taste for high living.

John Gauden was a native of Essex. At the time of his birth in 1605 his parents lived in the parish of Mayland, a few miles south of the Blackwater estuary, where his father was vicar. The young Gauden received his early education at Bury St. Edmunds school and then went to St. John's at Cambridge, where he took his B.A. in 1622 and his M.A. in 1625. There is no record of his admission to holy orders, but at some time during the next five years he married Elizabeth, daughter of Sir William Russell, Bart., of Chippenham, and widow of Edward Lewknow of Denham in Suffolk. In 1630 the Gaudens went to Oxford, where he attached himself to Wadham College and acted as tutor to his two young brothers-in-law, sons of Sir William. He remained at Oxford for 11 years, becoming a Bachelor of Divinity in July 1635 and a Doctor of Divinity on 8 July 1641.

Through his marriage into the Russell family, John Gauden gained his first foothold on the ladder of promotion which he was to climb with energetic determination to the end of his days. In March 1640 one of his former pupils, now Sir Francis Russell, presented him to the vicarage of Chippenham, a village not far from Newmarket in Cambridgeshire. This was soon augmented by an appointment as chaplain to the Earl of Warwick, an office which Gauden held simultaneously with the Chippenham living.

Robert Rich, the 2nd Earl of Warwick, was a dominant figure in 17th-century Essex. A staunch supporter of Parliament against the King, he was leader of the Puritan party and, having inherited from his great-grandfather the patronage of a number of livings in Essex, he was in a position to bestow them upon prominent Puritans in the county, usually people who were also prepared to act as his secret political agents. Gauden and many other priests were often entertained at his home, Leez Priory, six miles south-west of Bocking. This lovely manor, along with about a hundred others in Essex, had been acquired by the Earl's great-grandfather, the appropriately-named Lord Chancellor Rich, at the Dissolution. He had pulled down the original Priory and had built himself a magnificent brick mansion on the lines of Hampton Court, with an inner and an outer quadrangle. Water from the river Ter, which flowed through the garden, had been harnessed to feed artificial lakes and fountains. It was at Leez, in this beautiful setting, that John Gauden first experienced the pleasures of life in the grand manner.

Under Warwick's patronage, Gauden soon became a well-known figure in his own right. Although not entirely sympathetic to the Parliamentary views of his patron, he was skilful in concealing his true sentiments for the sake of personal advancement. He was appointed to preach before the House of Commons on 29 November 1640, an honour which brought him the gift of a large silver tankard inscribed '*Donum Honorarium populi Anglicani in parliamento Congregati, Johanni Gauden*'. The record of this gift is extant; the tankard itself has not been traced.

When the Deanery of Bocking became vacant in 1642, Warwick successfully influenced Parliament to nominate John Gauden for the office. Archbishop Laud, the legitimate patron, being then a prisoner in the Tower, was presumably required to give his formal assent.

Gauden immediately relinquished the living of Chippenham and took up residence at Bocking; he nevertheless remained at the beck and call of his patron and was in regular attendance at Leez. People were not slow to observe that he found the company there more to his taste than the weavers of his new parish. As Cuming Walters has put it, 'he was not distinguished for learning, eloquence, exceptional piety, or consistency' and although Parliament 'so far favoured the "trimming" parson as to appoint him Dean of Bocking . . . he had done little or nothing to make him worthy of that snug place . . .'.[35]

'Snug' as the Deanery may have been for the Calfhills and the Barkhams, the house was definitely not grand enough for Dr. and Mrs. John Gauden, and they soon set about improving it in accordance with their taste and the fashion of the day. Some major rebuilding of the roof was undertaken, probably before they took up residence. The leaded windows on the two centre gables also date from this time and still have their original wrought iron casement fittings. Many of the interior alterations and decorations made by the Gaudens have been covered or replaced in later 'renovations', but the Jacobean staircase remains. It is a beautiful piece of workmanship, and now that the many layers of paint have been stripped away it is restored to its former elegance.

At this date the front of the house still faced north-west, and it was here, below the present terrace, that Gauden is said to have planted the line of yews that have come to be known affectionately as 'the twelve Apostles'. Opinions vary as to the truth of the local tradition that Gauden planted the trees, for the bases of the yews are not large and doubt has been expressed as to their age. But it is remembered that they grew to a height of some 15 feet before they were cut back at the beginning of this century. One of the tasks of

Fig. 3

the Deanery gardeners has since been to keep the 'Apostles' in good shape.

So far as the Deanery garden is concerned, we can only guess at its appearance during Gauden's time. It was not laid out in its present form until a century later. We know that there was an orchard, and a pond between what is now the lawn and the adjacent laboratory buildings. There may also have been a walled garden, rose beds, a herb garden and shrubbery, and several paved walks. The English were just beginning to copy the Italians in designing fine gardens to match their fine houses.

At the back of the Deanery John Gauden built a dovecote with 135 nests. A plaster and lath construction on a brick sill, the lower timber-framed portion was probably then an open cart shed, the cote being reached by an outside ladder. It is still in its original place—obliquely south-west of what is today the front of the house, but the lower part has since been enclosed and framed by doors. In medieval times the privilege of keeping pigeons was granted only to lords of the manor and the clergy, but by the mid-17th century the custom had been adopted by most of the richer landowners. It is estimated that there were then about 26,000 dovecotes in England. Less than 500 remain nowadays, and Gauden's dovecote is one of less than 30 in Essex. Few of these still house pigeons, and none of them for food. There have been none at Bocking since the Second World War.

The original purpose of a dovecote was to ensure a steady supply of fresh meat to the household during the winter months. From Norman times until the introduction of root crops in the 18th century very few cattle could be fed all the year round, and the pigeon made a tasty substitute for the traditional roast beef. Those who were allowed to keep pigeons guarded their privilege most jealously, and penalties for infringements were very severe indeed: a pigeon thief was sometimes hanged for a third offence. No one bothered (or dared) to point out that the rich landowners' birds grew fat on other people's grain!

Adjoining the Deanery the Gaudens built a fair-sized coach house and extra stabling, all long since demolished. No doubt the Dean kept an elegant coach in harmony with his style of living, while his wife probably had a smaller one of her own in which she went visiting. We know that they were frequent guests of the Warwicks at Leez Priory, and we can be equally certain that the high-flying Dean saw to it that he and his wife were on visiting terms with all the great families of the county. They must also have entertained on a lavish scale at Bocking.

There is no doubt that Dean Gauden was an exceedingly wealthy man. The story is told that in a conversation between the Dean and Charles I, the King made the comment, 'Had

I but your wealth, Gauden, our country need not have been plunged into this sorrie Civil War!'

The contrast between 'high life' at the Deanery and the penurious state of some of the Bocking weavers at this time did not go unnoticed, and—as in the rest of England—much resentment grew among some sections of the population against the flamboyant wealth of the Church. Although a number of charities had been endowed in the parish at the beginning of the 17th century for the distribution of bread and money to the deserving poor, there was not enough to go round. In 1657 the local cloth trade, just beginning to recover from the great depression, suffered another terrible blow when Parliament imposed an additional duty on imported wines. Bocking and Braintree joined other Essex towns in a strongly-worded petition to Parliament:

> As our Bays, Says, Perpetuanos etc go Nine Tenths of them to Portugal and Spain, if a new Imposition be laid upon wines, the King of Portugal (we cannot but reasonably expect) then will prohibit our Manufactures . . . which will prove fatal to us as the Stagnation of the Blood. It will totally destroy the woollen Manufactury of Essex for 50 or 60,000 Families as Spinsters, Weavers and Combers, who are employed therein . . .[37]

In the event the new measures did not prove as disastrous as they feared, but no sooner had the trade begun to flourish again than the Great Plague swept through London and into Essex, killing thousands of people. It was to take a good 20 years for the master clothiers to recover from this setback, and it does them great credit that by the early 18th century the sales of 'Bockings', as the locally woven bays had come to be known, reached an unprecedented peak.

During the 17th century there was a shortage of small change, and many traders issued illegal tokens or 'money of necessity' to supplement the ordinary currency. Most of these trade tokens had the value of a halfpenny or a farthing. They usually bore the name or initials of the issuer and the name of the town, with some symbol representing the trade in which he was engaged. Thus the farthing of Abraham Ansell, Baker, has a

pair of scales and a wheatsheaf; that of Henry Ardley, Chandler,
a man making candles; while the halfpenny of Thomas Merill
the clothier bears his name and initials on one side of the
coin and the words 'in Bocking 1667—His Half Penny' on

Fig. 4

the other. These and similar tokens remained in circulation in the
district for 10 to 15 years.

The period that John Gauden spent at Bocking, 1642-1660,
was one fraught with intrigue and simmering rebellion. First
there was the Civil War and then, from 1649 onwards, the
troubled Commonwealth rule of Cromwell. Many of the Essex
gentry who had originally supported Parliament smartly switched
their allegiance to the Royalists as soon as they realised the
full implication of the New Order. The clergy were in a precarious
position: Cromwell had ordered that Puritan ministers were
to be appointed to all parish churches, and those who did not
conform ran the risk of forfeiting their livings at a moment's
notice. Gauden, as we have seen, was adept at keeping in with
both sides. In 1643 he was chosen as one of the Assembly of
Divines but was, as he himself wrote, shuffled out by a secret
committee and sleight of hand because he favoured regulating
rather than rooting out episcopacy. He is said to have taken
Cromwell's 'Solemn League and Covenant'—but went to great
pains thereafter to proclaim his Royalist views. He did
eventually conform to Presbyterianism in that he ceased to
use the English Prayer Book. This was 'abolished' by Parliament

in 1645, but was in use at Bocking longer than in most other churches.

While paying lip-service to Cromwell, the ambitious Dean was at the same time penning manuscript after manuscript protesting against the persecution of the Church and advancing the Royalist cause. These prolific writings were to earn him considerable promotion on the restoration of the monarchy, but at the time of publication such books as his *Religious and Loyal Protestation,* against the trial of Charles I, which appeared in 1649, must surely have endangered his life. In 1653 he wrote *A Defence by way of Apology for the Ministry and Ministers of the Church of England;* six years later he published a lengthy work under the title *The Tears, Signs, Complaints and Prayers of the Church of England: setting forth her former Constitution, compared with her present Condition: also the visible causes, and probable cures of her Distempers.* For all his faults—and who can blame a man for being ambitious? —John Gauden had courage.

Notoriety came to the Doctor towards the end of his life, when he was no longer at Bocking. In a letter dated 20 January 1661 to the Earl of Clarendon, then Lord Chancellor to Charles II, Gauden (who had just been made Bishop of Exeter) sought an even higher position in the Church, basing his claim on his alleged 'secret service'. This, he explained, had been the writing of the celebrated *Eikon Basilike: The Portraiture of His Sacred Majestie in his Solitudes and Sufferings,* which had caused a sensation when it appeared within a few hours of Charles I's execution in January 1649. At the time everyone believed the book to have been written by the King and it became immensely popular, running into nearly 50 editions within a year. Its impact on the English people at a moment of horror over the martyrdom of the King proved to be so potent a piece of propaganda for the Royalist cause that even the poet John Milton, engaged by the Puritans to reply, could do nothing effective against it.

Controversy over the authorship of *Eikon Basilike* lasted for many decades and has never been satisfactorily solved. Gauden himself wrote that he began the text in 1647. 'The book', he added, 'was wholly and only my invention in order to vindicate the King's wisdom and piety'. Bishop Christopher Wordsworth, writing in the 19th century,[38] was convinced that the King had written it. John Gauden, he said, was a 'cowering, craven, conceited, mean-spirited creature' totally incapable of having written 'anything before, or after, approaching to the *Eikon* in dignity and beauty'.

Other learned historians and bishops have argued the case: some that Gauden only remained silent for 10 years in the belief that he was thereby advancing the Royalist cause, others that a comparison between the style of his other writings and the *Eikon* throws grave doubts on Gauden as the author. It is true that by the time Gauden put forward his claim the monarchy had been restored and many of those who might have known the work's true authorship were no longer alive. Whereas Clarendon, replying to the Bishop's letter, admitted that he had been 'before acquainted with the secret' but 'had often wished he had remained ignorant of it'.

In 1692 there was published a treatise by Anthony Walker, the former curate and lifelong friend of the Gaudens, in support of the Doctor.[39] He maintained that Gauden, through the Marquess of Hertford, had sent the manuscript to the King at Carisbrooke where he was being held, but had retained a copy from which he published the book. More argument ensued, and if some of the stories then circulated are to be believed it is clear that whether or not Gauden actually wrote part or the whole of the book, on none of it, he was instrumental in getting it published and that much of the activity connected with this event must have taken place at Bocking.

There is one rather improbable story which purported that the King, on completing the manuscript, despatched it by messenger from Carisbrooke Castle to the printer in London. The royal emissary broke his journey overnight at Bocking, where the Dean begged to be allowed sight of the work. One of the deanery servants swore that he had been required to stay up all night long replenishing candles and making up the fire in Gauden's study while the Dean diligently copied out every word of the book before dawn. It was said that he made a number of amendments to the text as he worked, and subsequently claimed the whole to be his own composition. Unfortunately it does not seem very likely that a messenger hurrying to London from the Isle of Wight on urgent business for the King would go so far out of his way as to spend a night at Bocking.

Another version supports the theory that it was the King's work, but that it was edited and elaborated by Gauden. The Royal manuscript had somehow been entrusted to the care of the Rev. Edward Symmons, Minister of Rayne, near Braintree, it is thought through Lady Capel of Rayne Hall, whose husband, once a confidential servant of the King, was then in prison. Symmons, so the story goes, 'being interrupted by the troubles of his times, committed them [the papers] to his neighbour, Dr. Gauden, who, being a man of luxurious fancy, could not let them pass through his hands without amendments and additions'.[40] The Dean told Symmons that he had copied the text, ostensibly for his own private reading. Cleverly, as if by afterthought, he obtained Symmons's consent to substitute his copy for the King's own manuscript, on the plausible grounds that the Royal handwriting might be recognised and the book confiscated if it fell into the hands of any Parliamentarians.

Disaster almost did overtake the book at the eleventh hour. Symmons, while staying in Hertfordshire, had become involved with a lieutenant in a bitter quarrel concerning the way in which the army had treated the King. Threats were made, as a result of which Symmons fled to London, taking with him the previous manuscript and the proof sheets he was correcting for the printer. It happened that the young soldier's regiment, under the command of Colonel Rich, son of the Earl of Warwick, was also quartered in London, and a few days later he and Symmons came face to face. The lieutenant traced Symmons to his lodgings and ordered his men to enter the house and ransack his rooms. This they did very thoroughly and carried off most of the manuscript. The *Eikon* proofs were lying on the table, but the soldiers, apparently not realising that they were of any value, merely scattered them on the floor. Several sheets blew out of the open window and Symmons, who had escaped just in time, later picked them up in the street.

With great presence of mind the minister immediately informed Anthony Walker of the incident and begged him to use his influence with Colonel Rich to get the manuscript back. That evening Walker put on a wonderful act of the family chaplain asking a favour of his patron. The young lieutenant 'hath undone a poor parson in robbing him of his tools', he said. The Colonel succumbed and ordered that everything that had

been taken was to be restored to Symmons. Little did he realise
that what Walker had made out to be the minister's sermon
notes constituted some highly explosive writings.

Did Gauden write the *Eikon*? At least one historian comes
out strongly against:

. . . the testimonies which prove that performance to be
the King's are more numerous, certain and direct that
those of the other side. This is the case, even if we
consider the external evidence, but when we weigh the
internal, derived from the style and composition, there
is no matter of comparison. These meditations resemble
in elegance, purity, neatness and simplicity the genius
of those performances which we know with certainty
to have flowed from the Royal pen, but are so unlike
the bombastic, rhetorical and corrupt style of Dr. Gauden
that no human testimony seems sufficient to convince us
that he was the author . . .[41]

Some scholars have pointed out passages in the *Eikon* which
are very different in style from the main part of the work—
these, they say, may well have been added by John Gauden
to the Royal text.

The painful truth is that no one knows the answer. Bishop
Burnet, who once called *Eikon* 'the best writ book in the English
language', said:

There has been a great deal of disputing about the book:
some are so zealous for maintaining it to be the King's
that they think a man false to the Church that doubts
it to be his; yet the evidence since that time brought
to the contrary has been so strong, that I must leave
that under the same uncertainty under which I found
it; only this is certain, that Gauden never writ anything
with that force, his other writings being such that no
man, from a likeness of style, would think him capable
of writing so extraordinary a book as that is.[42]

There the matter rests. Either John Gauden wrote it and kept his authorship secret until such time as he could not resist the opportunity to use it for his personal advancement; or he waited until all those who knew the truth were dead and then deliberately laid claim to the King's work, again for his own gain. Perhaps the kindest thing to be said about this whole episode is that if Gauden did write the work, it is largely to him that we owe the restoration of a King to the throne of this country.

In any event, the Dean's work for the Royalist cause was to be amply rewarded by Charles II after the Restoration. In May 1660 he was made personal chaplain to the King and in November the same year he was appointed to the Bishopric of Exeter.

Gauden had spent 18 eventful years at Bocking, and he did not leave without making a generous gesture to the parish. He gave £400 to endow a school for the poor children, £100 of which was to be spent on a house in which the schoolmaster was to live and teach his pupils, and £300 to purchase lands to provide an income for the maintenance of the schoolmaster. The school, rebuilt at the beginning of the 20th century and named Gauden Hall, still exists in Church Lane, Bocking. The trust income (very low, of course, by modern standards) is administered by a panel of trustees, of which the Dean of Bocking is always chairman. Nowadays most of the funds are swallowed up by the rising costs of maintenance, but the trustees retain the right to make grants towards the further education of local children.

It was exactly one month after his elevation to Exeter that the Bishop wrote to Clarendon his famous letter complaining of the 'poverty' of that See (its revenues amounted to no less than £500 a year) and seeking a higher reward for his 'services'. Gauden had set his heart on becoming Bishop of Winchester.

That particular ambition was not achieved. When he saw that the vacancy at Winchester seemed imminent, Gauden pressed his claim once more, but to no avail. He went on pestering Clarendon and the Earl of Bristol for 15 months. In the end they gave him the Bishopric of Worcester, to which he was elected in May 1662. He died just four months later, on 20 September, following a violent attack of the stone and strangury which his enemies vowed had been brought on through vexation at missing Winchester. A monument and bust in Worcester Cathedral mark his resting place.

After her husband's death, Mrs. Gauden petitioned for a half year's share of the profits of Worcester, pleading the expense of their removal from Exeter. It was not allowed, for the reason that on his appointment to Exeter Gauden had received fines totalling £20,000. Thwarted in her demands, the good lady next claimed a remission of duty payable on her husband's estate, on the basis of his authorship of the *Eikon Basilike.*

They were a tough pair, the Gaudens. Bocking never saw their like again.

Richard Colebrand

The Restoration brought to Bocking a very different Dean. For Richard Colebrand not only had the signal honour of being appointed under the Royal Prerogative of Charles II (there was no Archbishop of Canterbury at the time, Laud having been executed in 1645): he was as modest as Gauden had been flamboyant and self-seeking.

Little is known of Colebrand's early career. He was a member of the Laudian clergy and in sympathy with the Archbishop's desire to restore decency and order in the Church. Like Laud, he had been brought up in comparatively humble circumstances and throughout his life remained aware of the sufferings of the poor. He was a scholar and Doctor of Divinity, a diligent, generous man who sought nothing more than the peace of God and the opportunity to lead a simple life. As chaplain to the King he had almost certainly shared the Royal exile in Holland, and it may have been as a reward for his loyalty during the King's misfortunes that Charles gave him the benefice of Bocking when it became vacant shortly after their return to England.

Colebrand came to the Deanery in December 1660 and remained in office until his death 14 years later. The records do not mention a wife, and his will refers only to nephews and nieces. But whether or not he had a family, of all the Bocking Deans up to this time he was the most loved by his parishioners. They knew him well, for the Dean employed no curate to help him with his parochial duties: he liked to go about among the people himself. He wrote up the parish registers in his own bold hand, and it is not difficult to imagine the sadness with which he recorded, one day in June 1666, 'Dyed of the Plague, 441'.

It was a distressing time, with whole families wiped out by the dreaded infection, and there were more deaths from the Plague in Bocking during the next few years, for although the Great Fire of London in September 1666 halted the spread of the disease in the City, the Plague then swept northwards and its after-effects were to be felt in Essex for years to come.

Dean Colebrand also held the living of Tippesfield, some eight miles north-west of Braintree. He exercised his ministry at a time of much strife and bitterness. In 1662 the new Book of Common Prayer was enforced, and dissenting clergy were ejected from their livings. Colebrand had always opposed the Puritan faction and insisted upon a reverent use of the Sacraments in his church. He also persuaded his parishioners to have their children baptised, which many had ceased to do. The Bocking registers reveal that during the Commonwealth only eight out of 500 infants born in the parish were baptised, whereas from 1661 onwards the baptisms more or less equalled the births.

The poor and destitute of the parish were assured not only of a sympathetic ear from their Dean, but of real practical help. Following Sunday morning service Colebrand personally supervised the distribution by the churchwardens of money and freshly-baked loaves of bread to those in most urgent need, as directed by the benefactors of those charities. He also gave generously himself to a new fund to provide fuel for the Bocking poor; he may even have instituted this particular charity. The churchwardens' accounts show that he was its most liberal supporter, for on 11 May 1671 they made an entry: 'Received of Doctor Colebrand thirty shillings to be added to the town or parish stock of wood money to buy wood for the poor'. And in his will the Dean bequeathed 'to the Church-wardens of the Parish of Bocking Ten pounds to add to their wood money, to buy in at the best hand in summer time wood for the poor and so to be sold out to them at the same price again in winter, and the stock to be preserved'. The charity flourished well into the 18th century.

His sympathies were not confined to those at home. According to the churchwardens' accounts, in 1670 he contributed generously to a charitable brief 'towards the ransoming of English men out of Turkish slavery' when a collection was made in the parish.

No record of Richard Colebrand's birth has been found, but it is assumed that he was at least in his middle years when he came to Bocking. By the summer of 1674 he was probably in his late sixties or early seventies. His health was failing, and on 23 August that year, only a few days before his death, the Dean made his will,[44] 'considering my owne frayle condition as alsoe I may have no worldly incumbrances upon my thoughts when it shall please God to call me from hence'. He gave detailed instructions for the distribution of his estate between nephews and nieces, friends, not forgetting the Deanery servants and the local poor, in order that, in his own words, 'I may not leave those blessings which I received from the God of peace subjects of strife and contention'. His body was to be placed at the north end of the Communion Table in the chancel of Bocking parish church, 'my executor to cause a Plate of Brasse to be fixed over the place with this inscription: HIC SUNT ILLIUS EXUVIAE QUI ASSIDUE ORAVIT PRO PACE ECCLESIAE [here lie the remains of one who prayed fervently for the peace of the Church].' To 'that servant whoever he bee that waites on me in my Chamber when I dye' he gave the sum of £3.

The Colebrand memorial is unique in that it does not bear the name of the departed. Such must have been the express wish of a modest man. And when some time after his death the Bocking blacksmith added a date to the memorial plate, he too respected the Dean's desire for anonymity. Only the Parish register records the burial: 'August 30th, Richard Colebrand, Dean and Rector'.

Itinerant Preacher

The Peace within the Church for which Colebrand had prayed was not yet in sight. Many of the dissenting clergy were

banding together and forming Nonconformist sects. Charles II
favoured the Catholic faith and issued an Act of Indulgence
which was promptly repealed by Parliament. His brother, James II,
on his accession tried hard to restore Roman Catholicism to
England, but met with formidable opposition. Meanwhile itinerant
Puritan preachers such as John Bunyan roamed the country
in between their long spells in gaol, inciting the masses to turn
from the Anglican doctrine. The struggle towards religious
tolerance promised to be not only bitter but protracted.

The Essex weaving towns were still going through a bad
time. In an attempt to protect the industry, an Act of Parliament
was passed in 1666 making it illegal to bury the dead (apart
from those who had died of the Plague) in any shroud not
made from pure sheep's wool. The first 'Burial in Woollen'
Act, as it was known, required the officiating clergyman
to sign an affidavit that the law had been complied with.
Its purpose was to discourage the use of imported linen and
to promote the sales of home-produced woollen cloth. However,
the Act was extensively evaded, in spite of further stringent
measures taken a few years later, for the wealthy preferred
to pay the £5 penalty for infringement rather than forego
the luxury of a softer shroud for their dear ones. And
since half the fine was repayable to the informant, many
families cleverly claimed back half the cost by informing on
themselves!

Very slowly the effects of the depression were overcome
and trade began to revive. By the last decade of the 17th
century Bocking was once more a prosperous town and many
of the local clothiers were amassing considerable fortunes to
hand down to their descendants. John Maysent, by his will
dated 10 June 1695, was able to leave to various members of
his family bequests totalling about £800, as well as property
and equipment.

In 1674 there came to the Deanery, in succession to
Dr. Colebrand, a dean about whom there is scanty biographical
detail. He was Nathaniel Sterry, brother of the better-known
Peter Sterry, chaplain to Cromwell. Nathaniel was also reputed
to have been an ardent Cromwellian. Educated at Emmanuel
College and later a Fellow of Merton College, Oxford, he was
a noted preacher and a scholar. Considering that he held office

at Bocking for 24 years, however, it is strange that no record
of this Dean has survived beyond the fact that he donated a
bell to the church. Even the memorial that once existed is
there no more.

There has long been a tradition locally that John Bunyan
wrote *Pilgrim's Progress* while staying at the house of the
English family at Bocking End. Both Sir William Addison
and the late Mr. Alfred Hills refer to his having preached
frequently in the square outside the *White Hart* inn and in
the great barn belonging to John English, the clothier.[45] It
is popularly believed that he was actually arrested while
preaching in Bocking in 1675, when he was committed to a
term of imprisonment in Bedford gaol. Most Bunyan experts
now agree that the latter part of the *Pilgrim* was written in the
years following Bunyan's release, 1676-7. During this period
Bunyan definitely stayed with the English family, and it is
more than likely that he worked at Bocking not only on that
book but also on the *Life and Death of Mr. Badman,* which
was published in 1680.

Another Bocking house in which Bunyan stayed was that
of John Tabor, who, together with his friend John English,
was a deacon of the Bocking Independent Meeting, an active
Nonconformist group which held regular gatherings in the
English barn. In 1707 a new Independent Meeting House was
built in place of the original barn. Renamed Bocking End Chapel,
it still stands today.

Bells and Bellringers

The Bocking churchwardens' accounts of this period are of
considerable interest. One entry for 20 July 1676 records the
payment 'to Thomas Daniel for mending the bells, 16s.'. And
on the same day, 'paid to the ringers for ringing when the King
came by, 12s.' Do we detect here a moment of panic when, with
the Royal procession nearing the town, the church bells were
found to be out of order?

Ringing the church bells on every conceivable occasion—
religious and otherwise—had been customary since the Middle
Ages. The medieval English were merry people at heart: they
loved to celebrate, to feast and to dance. The menfolk (and

particularly the bellringers, for change-ringing was thirsty work) loved their ale. So they rang the bells at the slighest excuse, whether it was a religious festival, a wedding, the harvest supper, or whenever the King or some other eminent personage rode through the town. When there was no other reason to indulge their pastime, they organised bell-ringing contests with teams from nearly parishes. And every time they rang the bells at Bocking, the 'ringers' jug' would be passed round to collect ale for the hard-working ringers.

These jugs, which were peculiar to Essex, sometimes held as much as four and a half gallons of ale. They were usually kept in the inn nearest to the church—in this case at the *Six Bells*— where the men would foregather after their stint was done. It was not uncommon for parishioners to bequeath money for the bells to be rung on a particular anniversary, and this normally included the provision of ale for the ringers.

The old inn which stood on the site of the medieval hospice of St. James must have taken its name from the Bocking bells, of which there were six at this time. Two of the old peal have been long since replaced. Of the remaining four, the earliest in date are a pair (now the third and fourth bells) cast by John Darbie of Ipswich, a famous founder who cast 19 bells for Essex churches. These two bells are engraved with his name and the date 1682, with the initials 'J. W.'), believed to indicate their donor, probably John Wall, a Bocking glover. The fifth bell is also by Darbie and is dated 1685. Dean Sterry is said to have given the sixth, which came from a well-known Whitechapel foundry and bears the inscription, 'JAMES BARTLETT MADE ME 1682 JOHN MARYON DANIELL TREE CHURCHWARDENS' and below this the Bartlett trade-mark, three bells within a circle. It is one of eight bells which Bartlett made for Essex.

The Whitechapel foundry where Bartlett worked became famous many years later under Mears and Stainbank, who recast the bell of Big Ben in 1858. The same firm also cast the two bells added to the Bocking peal in 1856, and another two in 1904.

Bocking bells and the men who rang them have been famous in Essex for generations. When change-ringing was revived in the mid-19th century, St. Mary's became *the* fashionable church

for weddings in the district, and many Braintree people are
said to have deposited their suitcases at Bocking in order to
fulfil the statutory residence requirements. (In all fairness it
must be added that the Braintree bells were at this time
damaged and silent.) A certain friendly
rivalry has continued into the 20th
century, however, for as soon as the Braintree ring was increased to eight, Bocking
followed suit.[46]

To return to those 17th century ringers,
how fascinating it would be to eavesdrop
on their conversation at the *Six Bells*!
What, for instance, would they have had
to say about 'Old Harkilees', the strange
carved figure which is said to have been
their mascot but which now looks down
at passers-by from above the doorway of
the modern public house called *The Six
Bells*?

'Old Harkilees' is a Bocking celebrity.
Many a local child has listened spellbound
to parent or grandparent recounting the
legend that as soon as the church clock
strikes midnight Harkilees goes down to
the river for a drink, or— according to
another version—for a swim. Some apparently credulous children once mounted a
night watch in the hope of observing the
strange legless creature in the act. They
returned home disappointed, proclaiming
Harkilees to be stone deaf, since he did
not appear to have heard the chimes and had made no move.

Where did he come from, and why did he once preside like
a gargoyle above the rainwater pipe on the *Six Bells* inn?
For a long time he was simply propped up against the front
of the building, and it is within living memory that he was
elevated to the upper storey. The old inn then stood much
closer to the junction of Bradford Street and Church Lane
than the present house. When it was demolished as part of
a road-widening scheme in the mid-1920s, Harkilees was salvaged

and eventually placed above the entrance to the modern building. Some people have tried to connect him with John Gauden, pointing out the figure's curious resemblance to King Charles I. A more probable explanation is that he once formed part of the surround of a large Tudor fireplace and that he was thrown out of his original home at a time of restoration, adopted by the Bocking bellringers and borne off to the inn in triumph. It may not be a coincidence that there were in the early 17th century two houses within a stone's throw of the inn owned by men with the name of Hercules: one in Church Lane built by a wealthy clothier, Hercules Stevens, the other a manor house called Fryers in Bradford Street, the home of Hercules Arthur. If the carving originated from one of these fine houses, what could be more natural than that the bellringers should christen him 'Old Harkilees'?

What more natural either than that those same St. Mary's bellringers should one winter's day in 1698 ring out a peal in celebration of the most popular appointment ever made to Bocking Deanery?

'For ringing the bells at the coming of Sir Will, four shillings and ninepence', duly recorded the churchwardens. It was not their place to describe the joy in everyone's heart, nor how much ale was drunk in the local inns on that occasion. But it was something that Bockonians were not likely to forget for a very long time.

'Sir Will'

Sir William Dawes was a favourite at the Court. He was also one of the most popular pulpit orators of his day in England, and the Essex people honoured him as the son and heir of one of their most distinguished families. At Bocking they took 'Sir Will' to their hearts for the simple reason that he was *their* man.

He came to the Deanery a wealthy young man of 28, already a Doctor of Divinity (conferred on him by Royal Mandate while he was too young to take it normally) and having recently been unamimously elected to the Mastership of St. Catherine's Hall, Cambridge. On his mother's as well as on his father's side the family held large estates in Essex, and Sir William had recently married Frances, eldest daughter of Sir Thomas D'Arcy of Braxted Lodge also in the county.

The Dawes family seat was Lyons Hall, a manor adjoining Bocking and lying between the Four Releet and Stisted. It had come into the family through his mother, one of the Hawkyns of Braintree, and it was here in August 1671 that William was born. He was the third son of Sir John Dawes, on whom Charles II had at the Restoration bestowed a baronetcy 'in memory of many services conferred, and hardships undergone by the family in the civil confusion, and in acknowledgement of several sums of money annually transmitted to the Royal family in exile'. During the Civil War, by reason of their attachment to the Royalist cause, the Dawes family had forfeited much of their inherited estates.

Young Will was a precocious child. Sent to Merchant Taylors' School at the age of nine, he became a classical scholar and by his 15th birthday had also mastered Hebrew. Two elder brothers having died while he was up at St. John's College, Oxford, he was now heir to the family fortune. He took his deceased eldest brother's place at St. Catherine's Hall, Cambridge.

Too young to take holy orders, on which he had set his mind, Sir William next spent some time touring his estates. During his travels he met and fell in love with the girl who later became his wife. Honours followed in rapid succession. In 1696 he was appointed chaplain-in-ordinary to William III. On 5 November the same he year he preached before the King at Whitehall a sermon which so pleased His Majesty that he made Dawes a Prebendary of Worcester Cathedral. The following year he became Master at St. Catherine's Hall and a year after that Vice-Chancellor of Cambridge University.

As a country squire he was immensely popular. When Dean Sterry died in 1698 a number of local people expressed a wish to petition the Archbishop to appoint 'Sir Will' to the vacancy. This Dawes refused to allow them to do, but Archbishop Tenison must have got wind of their plan and approved it, for he promptly collated Sir William to the Rectory of Bocking, and on 19 December commissioned him as Dean.

It is thought that Dawes built on to the Deanery the decorative gable and façade which is now the front of the house. The internal entrance doors and the archway leading to the domestic quarters may have been added at the same time, as well as some of the ground-floor panelling, the moulded ceilings and fine fireplaces.

While the builders were at work the Dean probably continued to live at Lyons Hall. In fact, with the family estate so close, it is unlikely that Sir William and his wife spent much time in residence at the Deanery. Nevertheless it is on record that 'his life at Bocking was that of a good country parson; every Sunday he invited 'some of the better sort' to dine with him; and he established at once a monthly celebration of the Holy Communion, which before his time had only been celebrated at the three great festivals'.

Dawes's reputation as a preacher is said to have been due to 'the comeliness of his person, the melody of his voice, the appropriateness of his action, and the majesty of his whole appearance'.[47] On one occasion he lost preferment to the Bishopric of Lincoln because a bold sermon given before the Queen incurred the displeasure of some influential men at Court. To the nobleman who informed him of this, Sir William apparently retorted that 'as to that, he had no manner of concern upon him, because his intention was never to gain one [a bishopric] by preaching'.[48] Queen Anne herself, who on accession to the throne had made Sir William one of her chaplains and looked on him as a great favourite, seems not to have been displeased at all. Much to the annoyance of the Whig element at Court, in 1707 she nominated Dawes to the See of Chester.

Bocking was reluctant to let him go. Presumably he was prevailed on to continue at the Deanery, for during the next few years he held office simultaneously as Bishop of Chester and Dean of Bocking. But in 1714, following a deathbed recommendation made by Archbishop Sharp, Dawes was appointed Archbishop of York and was obliged to take up permanent residence at Bishopthorpe. When the Queen died in the summer of that year, he was called upon to act as one of the Regents pending the arrival in England of the new King, George of Hanover. In fact Dawes was to spend only 10 years in Yorkshire. He died on 30 April 1724 and was buried beside his wife in the chapel of his beloved St. Catherine's Hall at Cambridge.

Although Sir William was Dean of Bocking for only 15 years, he had the satisfaction of leaving the parish in a happier state than when he came to it. There was now greater stability and order in the Church, as well as a new prosperity in the local cloth trade. The Deanery was at its most elegant; and in the church were several treasures which are believed to have been his gifts—a silver flagon and stand-platen of 1700, a silver alms-dish of 1704, the two upholstered and elaborately-carved chairs now in the Sanctuary, and the handsome table with the twisted legs that stands in the sacristy.

Dawes was also a generous benefactor to St. Catherine's Hall, to which he left a considerable amount of money. But the bulk of his estate passed to his granddaughter, Elizabeth. It has been written that Sir William Dawes was an ancestor of the present Earl of Harewood. This is incorrect. Elizabeth married Edwin Lascelles, Member of Parliament for Yorkshire, who was created 1st Baron Harewood in 1790. It was a childless marriage. Although the Baron remarried after Elizabeth's death, he died without issue and was succeeded in the title by his cousin Edward, from whom the present line of Harewoods are directly descended.

Uneventful Decade

Three Deans held office during the next 10 years: Robert Clavering, William Beauvoir and Robert Wake. None of them stayed long or achieved anything spectacular in the parish, although Beauvoir had led a colourful life before coming to Bocking.

Dean Clavering, who succeeded Dawes in 1714, maintained the tradition of the scholar incumbent. A Fellow and Tutor of University College, Oxford, and Doctor of Divinity, he was elected Regius Professor of Hebrew in that University in 1715, an appointment which he held to the end of his life.

In 1719, after only four years at Bocking, he resigned to take the well-endowed rectory of Marsh-Gibbon in Buckinghamshire. Advancement followed rapidly. He was appointed chaplain to the Archbishop of Canterbury while at Marsh-Gibbon, and in January 1725 became Bishop of Llandaff and Dean of Hereford. In February 1729 he was appointed to the See of Peterborough. Clavering was Bishop of Peterborough for nearly 20 years; he died in 1747 holding four offices, having obtained speicial permission to retain his professorship, his prebend and the rectory of Marsh-Gibbon along with the Bishopric.

By contrast, William Beauvoir, the next Dean, came to Bocking in his 50th year with an unusual naval career behind him. Born in Guernsey, the only son of Peter de Beauvoir and Anne Le Hardy, he had taken his B.A. at Pembroke College, Oxford, in 1691. The following year he returned to Guernsey as Rector of St. Saviour's Church. The register of that church records his appointment on 21 June 1692 and the fact that he preached his first sermon there on 2 July. It then states three years later, that 'Mr. William de Beauvoir went away in one of his Majesty's frigates'—and there is no record of his ever returning to the parish, although he continued to hold the rectory until his death in 1724.

Apparently a de Beauvoir relation on his mother's side, Captain Thomas Le Hardy, was at that time stationed in Guernsey with the 18-gun *Swallow Prize,* one of two frigates of the British Navy sent out at the island's request to give protection and to safeguard trade with England. The captain must have so fired the Rector of St. Saviour's with enthusiasm for the seafaring life that when Le Hardy was given command of the 48-gun *Pendennis* in September 1695 and left the island, de Beauvoir sailed with him—presumably as naval chaplain or captain's secretary.

His service with the Navy was not without excitement, for de Beauvoir seems to have played an important rôle in the capture of the Franco-Spanish fleet at Vigo in 1702. By that time Le Hardy was in command of the *Pembroke*, which had 64 guns. In October 1702, while watering at Lagos, on the south coast of Portugal, a party from the frigate went ashore and through de Beauvoir's command of French managed to establish excellent relations with the French Consul. When the Consul let slip a casual remark at some social function to the effect that the French fleet was ensconced in Vigo Bay, de Beauvoir went straight to Captain Le Hardy, who in turn lost no time in rejoining the main fleet then cruising off the coast under Sir George Rooke. A combined British and Dutch fleet destroyed the Franco-Spanish ships in the Bay, and Rooke entered Vigo, capturing galleons carrying gold and silver treasure worth more than a million pounds.

De Beauvoir must have received a share of the considerable prize money. He left the Navy soon afterwards, but seems to have had no wish to return to his living in Guernsey, for in 1704 he took his M.A. degree at Corpus Christi, Cambridge, and subsequently went to live in Paris, where he became chaplain to the British Ambassador, the Earl of Stair. There he played a prominent part in the negotiations which were conducted during 1718-18 between the Archbishop of Canterbury and Doctors of the Sorbonne concerning a possible union between the English and Gallican churches. Records containing a number of letters between Archbishop Wake and de Beauvoir on this subject have survived, and it is likely that when the Deanery of Bocking fell vacant in 1719 it was granted to de Beauvoir in recognition of his services during these negotiations.

One of the first things the new Dean did on taking up his appointment was to anglicise his name. From this time on he appears in the records as 'William Beauvoir'. He probably married a young wife on his return to England, for a son, Osmund, was born to him at Bocking in October 1721; the baptismal entry in the parish register is in the Dean's own handwriting. Less than three years later, in February 1723/4,[49] William Beauvoir died. As the register records, he was buried at Bocking.

The next incumbent was even more short-lived than his two predecessors. So brief was his term of office at Bocking— barely two and a half years—that we know nothing of him except his name, Robert Wake. By contrast, the Dean who followed him, John Walker, left behind some notebooks[50] which have been preserved; they provide a fascinating picture of the age. He also left his mark on the Deanery grounds, still visible today. As his methodically-detailed accounts record, the greater part of the garden was laid out under his guidance. Thus the name of John Walker must be linked with James Calfhill, John Gauden and Sir William Dawes, all of whom made significant improvements to the Deanery in their time.

Dean Walker

John Walker was collated to the Rectory and Deanery of Bocking by Archbishop Wake[51] in November 1725. He came from Paris, where he had been the emissary of a well-known

classical scholar of the day, Richard Bentley, with whom he
was working on a collection of Graeco-Latin Testaments. This
work had led to Walker's friendship with the Archbishop.
Unfortunately the edition was never published, for both editors
were to die within a few months of one another, Walker at the
age of 48, in 1741.

The new Dean was another in the line of eminent scholar
incumbents. Educated at Wakefield School, in 1710 he had
entered Trinity College, Cambridge, where he was considered
'amiable and attractive, ready to work with others, as well as
learned'; he became a Fellow of the College in 1717, the year
in which he took his M.A. On 26 January 1727/8, just over
a year after his appointment to Bocking, Walker married
Charlotte Sheffield, one of three natural daughters of John
Sheffield, 1st Duke of Buckingham and Normanby. Her father
had died in 1721, and under the terms of his will the girls
had taken the name of Sheffield. Charlotte, who is said to
have been 'a woman of violent and turbulent temper', brought
to her husband a fortune of £6,000. She bore him six sons and
four daughters, six of whom survived their father. The Deanery
house and grounds must have resounded during these years with
the voices and laughter of children.

In common with the practice of clergy at this time, John
Walker held several posts concurrently with Bocking. He became
Chancellor of St. Davids, in Wales, in 1727, and a Doctor of
Divinity in April 1728. The following year, Archbishop Wake
made him Archdeacon of Hereford; in December 1730 he was
given the Rectory of St. Mary Aldermary in London, and in
1732 the living of St. Thomas the Apostle in the City. In addition
to these many duties, he also acted as chaplain to King George II,
who had acceded in 1727.

It was the 'Age of Elegance' in England. Architecture, music,
painting and literature flourished; the gentry prided themselves
on their fine clothes and the excellence of their table; landed
families spent colossal sums on building magnificent mansions
encircled by landscaped parks and gardens. Walker seems to
have shared this fashionable interest in gardens, for in August
1730 he called in a Mr. Robert Addison to survey the grounds
surrounding 'Bocking Parsonage', as the Dean always called
the Deanery. In his notebooks he invariably refers to the garden

as 'the Orchard', which may indicate that when he came to live at Bocking the greater proportion of the grounds was given over to fruit trees.

Addison's survey showed that 'the Orchard' extended over 1 acre, 3 roods and 21 poles, of which 'the Pond' occupied 9 poles and 'the Wilderness' 28 poles, leaving 1 acre, 2 roods and 24 poles of ground which could be cultivated.[52] From Walker's account book of 1733–4 we learn that he spent a considerable amount of money on hedging and laying out the Deanery grounds. His pride and joy seems to have been 'the Great Walk in the Orchard' which he planted with the lovely lime trees we admire today, a loyal tribute to his Hanoverian monarch; the Stuarts had planted firs. The accounts contain many items relating to his work:

			£	s.	d.
1733	Dec. 14	Pd. for making the ditch & hedge for the Orchard· ..	1	11	8
		Pd. the Labourers for work in the great Walk in the Orchard	3	2	0
	19 Dec.	Pd. Tansley the gardener for the walk, box, & Horn-beam etc.	4	9	6
1733/4	15 Jan^y	Pd. Tansley for trees, goose-berry bushes, etc. & work		19	6
	and				
1734	from 25 May to June 27 ..	pd. for stubbing gravel, making the Walk, etc. ..	7	1	2½

There are other entries of expenditure on what the Dean calls 'Quick Hedge' or 'Quickset Hedge', and gravel for the walk and forecourt. On 30 May 1738 he records a payment 'for ditching, hedging and quicks for the grass walk, 1-11-2.' It is interesting to read that a labourer or gardener then earned, for two-and-a-half days' work, the princely sum of 2s. ·8d. For 'working by the day' Walker records paying out the 'Thatcher, 1/6, Ale 2d' and '2 Labourers, 2/-, Ale 4d', which he calculated as 'per square 3/0, more, Ale 4d'.

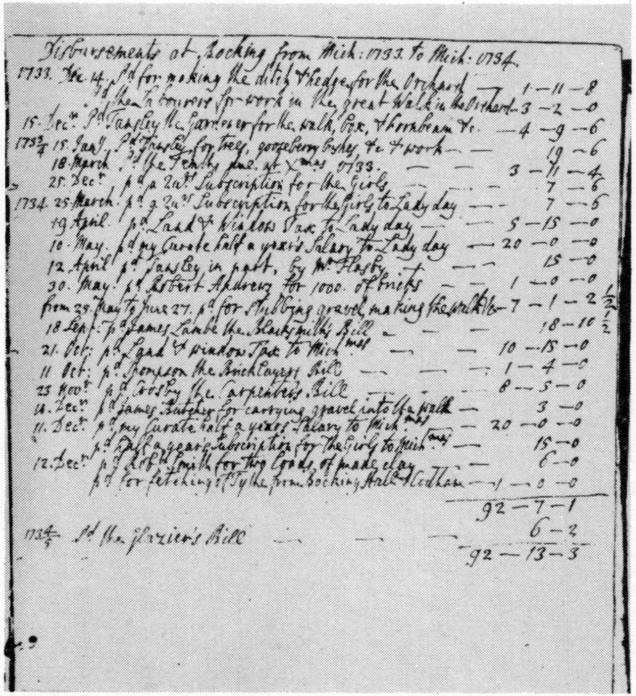

Disbursements at Bocking from Mich: 1733 to Mich: 1734.

1733. Dec. 14. pd for making the ditch & hedge for the Orchard		1 — 11 — 8
pd them [illegible] for work in the great Walk in the Orchard		3 — 2 — 0
15. Decr. pd Tansley the Gardener for the walk, box, & hornbeam &c.		4 — 9 — 6
1733/4 15. Jan. pd Tansley for trees, gooseberry bushes, &c & work		19 — 6
18. March. pd the Tenths due at Xmas 1733.		3 — 11 — 4
25. Decr. pd a 2nd Subscription for the Girls		7 — 6
1734. 25. March. pd a 2nd Subscription for the Girls to Lady day		7 — 6
19 April. pd Land & Window Tax to Lady day		5 — 15 — 0
10. May. pd my Curate half a year's Salary to Lady day		20 — 0 — 0
12. April. pd Tansley in part, by Mr Flasby		15 — 0
30. May. pd Robert Andrews for 1000. of bricks		1 — 0 — 0
from 28. May to June 27. pd for stubbing gravel, making the walk &c		7 — 1 — 2 1/2
18 Sept. pd James Lambe the Blacksmith's Bill		18 — 10 1/2
21. Oct. pd Land & window Tax to Michmas		10 — 15 — 0
11 Oct. pd Thompson the Bricklayer's Bill		1 — 4 — 0
23 Novr. pd Crosby the Carpenter's Bill		8 — 5 — 0
14. Decr. pd James Butcher for carrying gravel into the walk		3 — 0
11. Decr. pd my Curate half a year's Salary to Michmas		20 — 0 — 0
pd half a year's Subscription for the Girls to Michmas		15 — 0
12. Decr. pd Robt Smith for two Loads of made clay		6 — 0
pd for fetching ye Tythe from Bocking Hall [illegible]		1 — 0 — 0
		92 — 7 — 1
1734/5 pd the Glazier's Bill		6 — 2
		92 — 13 — 3

Fig. 5

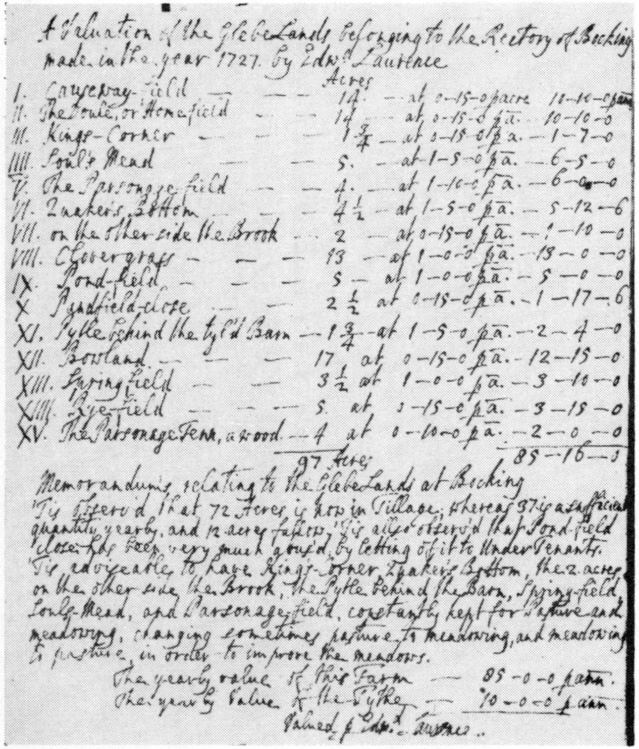

A Valuation of the Glebe Lands belonging to the Rectory of Bocking made in the year 1727. by Edwd Laurence

	Acres		
I. Causeway-field	14	at 0—15—0 p acre	10—10—0 p ann
II. The Soule, or Home-field	14	at 0—15—0 p a.	10—10—0
III. Kings-Corner	1 3/4	at 0—15—0 p a.	1—7—0
IIII. Soul's Mead	5.	at 1—5—0 p a.	6—5—0
V. The Parsonage-field	4.	at 1—10—0 p a.	6—0—0
VI. Quaker's Bottom	4 1/2	at 1—5—0 p a.	5—12—6
VII. on the other side the Brook	2	at 0—15—0 p a.	1—10—0
VIII. Clover grass	13	at 1—0—0 p a.	13—0—0
IX. Pond-field	5	at 1—0—0 p a.	5—0—0
X. Pondfield-close	2 1/2	at 0—15—0 p a.	1—17—6
XI. Pyghtle behind the tyth Barn	1 3/4	at 1—5—0 p a.	2—4—0
XII. Bowland	17	at 0—15—0 p a.	12—15—0
XIII. Springfield	3 1/2	at 1—0—0 p a.	3—10—0
XIIII. Rye-field	5.	at 0—15—0 p a.	3—15—0
XV. The Parsonage Fenn, a wood	4	at 0—10—0 p a.	2—0—0
	97 Acres		85—16—0

Memorandums relating to the Glebe Lands at Bocking
'Tis observ'd that 72 Acres is now in Tillage, whereas 37 is a sufficient quantity yearly, and 12 acres fallow. 'Tis also observ'd that Pond-field close has been very much abus'd by letting of it to Under Tenants. 'Tis adviseable to have Kings-Corner, Quaker's Bottom, the 2 acres on the other side the Brook, the Pyghtle behind the Barn, Spring-field, Soule-Mead, and Parsonage-field, constantly kept for pasture and meadowing, changing sometimes pasture to meadowing, and meadowing to pasture, in order to improve the meadows.

The yearly value of this Farm — 85—0—0 p ann.
The yearly Value of the Tythe — 70—0—0 p ann.

Valued p Edwd Laurence.

Fig. 6

There may have been more notebooks; the two that have
survived contain a mass of information about the Deanery
and the benefice, but tell us nothing of Walker's work in the
parish or church. Curiously enough, although he was a classical
scholar, he seems to have been fascinated by the problems of
algebra, which take up several pages. But whatever else he was,
the Dean was both meticulous and methodical: he set down
not only all his expenses and receipts from tithes, but made
tables showing how the glebe lands were farmed, noting the
crops in each field in a given year. One typical book is headed,
on the title page: 'J. Walker 1730. Several Particulars relating
to the Rectory of Bocking: Collected with Expense and trouble,
and cast into the following Method in order for farther Improvements . . .'.

James Butcher, who was the tenant of Glebe Farm during
Walker's incumbency, paid the Dean £75 a year in rent, For the
rest, the 'true rent' or value of each holding was carefully
noted, together with the amount paid in Land Tax (2s. in the £)
and what the Dean calls the 'Poors' Rate' This seems to have
been very heavy, for Richard Joslin of Bovington Farm paid
£64 a year and Sam Tabor £42 for Ayletts' Farm, relatively
large sums for the period.

The bulk of the Dean's income came from the tithes, and
Walker kept a detailed record of each farm and holding, noting
also whether his tithe payers were Churchmen or Dissenters.
Usually he differentiated between Quakers and Dissenters, but
sometimes just wrote 'Church' or 'goes nowhere'. Of 44 tithe
payers noted, 26 were 'Churchmen', 15 Dissenters or Quakers,
and three 'went nowhere'.

The tithes were mostly paid in cash, although occasionally
the Dean had a private agreement with the tenant to accept
payment in kind, often in wood. Bocking must have been
surrounded by woods in the 18th century, and according to
Walker's notebooks some of them had attractive names: Pampling
Spring, Pimpernel Spring, Dols Hole, Harris Grove . . . Each
tithe payer had a separate agreement with the Dean, signed
and witnessed, setting out a fixed payment for a fixed number
of years. Sometimes in addition to the money tithe the tenant
agreed to supply the Dean with a stated quantity of hops, or to
provide a certain service, such as to fetch him a waggonload

of coals once a year. At the foot of the agreement made in December 1729 with Thomas Ruggles (an ancestor of the Present Colonel Sir John Ruggles-Brise, Bart., Lord Lieutenant of Essex), for the tenancy of a farm called Bradfords at £4 10s. per annum, the Dean added a note: 'That I have promised to take four pounds & five shillings for the Tythe of it if Mr. Ruggles assures me upon his word that it is not worth four pounds & ten shillings. J. Walker'. He was a fair man.

The tenant of Bovington promised to furnish the Dean with 20 pounds of his 'best bright hops', and another, of Codham Hall, was to pay annually the sum of £6 6s. and a further sum of £1 sterling and 12 pounds' weight of good hops for the hop ground.

According to Walker, 26 acres were devoted to growing hops at Bocking at this time, and 112 cwt. were produced in the year. The Dean evidently brewed his own ale, for his notebooks are full of expenses in this connection: the purchases of malt, additional hops and hogsheads (these held 54 gallons each). In an inventory of 'Some things belonging to me at the Parsonage at Bocking' made in 1729 he lists 'two half hogsheads, more, four half hogsheads, more, two half hogsheads . . . two Ale stalls in the Cellar', adding that he bought these from Mrs. Wake, the widow of his predecessor. It has been calculated that if the Dean filled all these casks he would have had 270 gallons of ale. Apparently this was insufficient to quench his household's thirst, for in 1728 he bought two more hogsheads 'new' at a price of 16s. and another two half hogsheads 'secondhand' which cost him 13s.

Once a year the Dean entertained his tithe payers to what he calls 'The Tythe Feast' held at the *White Hart* inn. The accounts show that this usually cost him just over £3, which he paid to the innkeepers, Daniel and Elias Trew.

As well as his income from tithes and the glebe farm, the Dean recorded all the fees he received for various services performed in the parish. 'For Registering a child baptiz'd, 6 pence to the Rector . . .'. 'Marriage. For Publishing the Banns, A Shilling, half to the Rector, & half to the Clark . . . For marrying with Publication, half a Crown to the Rector, a Shilling to the Clark . . .'. 'Buryings. Burial of Persons above 16 years old, 1s-0, under that Age, 6d., extraparochial persons, double. Leading Prayers of a Funeral, 5s-0 . . .'. 'For placing, or replacing, two Stones or two wooden Posts in the Church Yard at each End of a Grave, 10s-6d. to the Rector . . .:. 'For breaking ground in the Chancel, £1-1-0 . . . For a brick grave in the Churchyard, 10-6'.

Altogether John Walker probably received a net income from the Rectory of around £400 a year, out of which he had to pay Land and Window Tax amounting to £30 a year (no wonder several of the windows at the Deanery were blocked in!) and a stipend to his curate of about £40, plus sundry bricklayers', carpenters' and glaziers' bills for the upkeep of the house and the chancel of the church. He also paid regularly every quarter the sum of 7s. 6d. 'for teaching the Girls'. This was probably for the tutoring of his own daughers, rather than for a parish school for girls. There is no record of a girls' school at Bocking before 1812.

Private wealth enabled the Walkers to live in refined luxury at the Deanery, and they must have entertained a good deal there. They would not have lacked servants, and like most of the gentry of their day they spent lavishly on elegant furnishings for the house, especially on fine porcelain and silverware to grace their dinner table. Some of the Walker armorial dinner service still exists. Now part of a private collection, it was once in regular use at Bocking.

John Walker died on 9 November 1741, at the relatively young age of forty-eight. Whether he was worn out by the demands of his several offices and a hot-tempered wife, or whether he contracted some fatal disease, the records do not reveal. For all her faults Mrs. Walker had great respect for her husband, coupled with an acute awareness of her own shortcomings. On the memorial stone in the chancel of the parish church she had put up, in the rather excruciatingly fulsome style of the day, the following tribute to a man

> Whose uncommon learning and sweetness of Temper joined to all other perfections and accompany'ed with a Pleasing Form of Body had justly rendered him the Delight and Ornament of Mankind . . . Universally regretted by the Ingenious, the good and the Polite . . .

This plaque, once on the floor of the chancel, is now high on the north wall.

A Curate's Record

During the last four and a half years of his life, Dean Walker was fortunate in having the assistance of an able young curate by the name of John Cutler.

In the absence of biographical documentation, we assume that the curate was young at the time he took up his duties in Bocking, since he remained in the parish for no less than 43 years, an exceptionally long curacy by any standards. The appointment was probably the first of Cutlers's ecclesiastical career. By the time it ended, and he left to become Vicar of Cressing, near Braintree, he had made himself indispensable to three Deans in succession; he was also something of an institution in Bocking, a familiar figure to be seen daily riding on horseback down Church Street and along the country lanes about his, or rather, the Dean's, business, visiting the poor and the sick, collecting tithes and distributing alms. To the ordinary folk, who were much in awe of the great Dean, Cutler was spiritual adviser, friend and comforter. To the masters he served, he was a loyal servant on whom they could rely to see that routine parochial matters were attended to while they busied themselves with grander affairs in London or elsewhere.

To Cutler we owe most of our knowledge of the parish during these years, for there are virtually no records of the next two Deans he served: George Sayer, who succeeded Dr. Walker and held office for 20 years, and Charles Hall, D.D., who succeeded Sayer in October 1761. Happily the curate kept methodical accounts, and two of his notebooks, covering the years 1737-62, have been preserved.[53] If there was a third book, kept during Cutler's last eight years at Bocking, this unfortunately has not survived. It may never have existed: Dr. Hall, who became Dean in 1761, may have preferred to handle all the records personally.

Cutler must have started keeping the books within days of his arrival at Bocking, in midsummer 1737, for the first page is headed: 'Surplice Fees in Bocking from June 28th, 1737, to Michaelmas do.'. It is not difficult to detect here the influence of Dean Walker, who perhaps summoned the new curate to the Deanery to instruct him upon his duties and took the opportunity of impressing upon him the wisdom of keeping methodical records. Certainly Cutler seems to have been a model pupil, for his accounts are as beautifully kept as the Dean's, and in a very neat handwriting. All fees received are listed, as well as the Easter Offerings, records of the distribution of alms at Holy Communion, and details of the monies collected for the many 'Briefs' received by the parish at this time. These were letters patent issued by the Sovereign for the purpose of raising money in various parts of the country to help churches in need of repair, or parishes that had suffered a major disaster, such as fire or flood. The curate even includes details of what it cost him to keep his horse—around £7 a year, an expense which he must sometimes have found it difficult to meet out of his slender stipend of £50 per annum.

It was customary for a curate to take the fees for the services he performed, which in Cutler's day meant 6d. for registering a baptism, 2s. 6d. for a wedding, 6d. for a burial—or 6s. if the body was brought into church for a full funeral service, and he also collected the Easter Offerings from all houses in the parish, usually at the rate of 2d. per head for each person of 16 years and over. The Dean would then make up the balance to the curate's agreed total stipend.

There were ways and means of supplementing the curate's income, and sometimes the more generous Deans would see to it that he received the present of a guinea or two at intervals during the year—Dr. Sayer quite often rewarded Cutler in this manner, probably for extra services rendered during his absence. Then the curate might earn another few pounds by collecting the Rector's tithes for him, or by transacting business connected with the Registry of the Deanery—usually proving a will. Preaching a funeral sermon occasionally brought in another 10s., paid by the 'Funeral Sermon Society', and there are a number of entries in the book of fees Cutler received for 'Gloves' (2s. 6d.), 'Hatbands and Gloves' (8s. 6d.), and 'Scarf and Hatband and Gloves' (£1 4s. 6d.), which presumably also relate to funerals and went towards the purchase, and laundering, of these items of clothing which were required to be worn on important occasions. Funerals seem to have accounted for the bulk of his income.

Master Clothiers

Apart from a short period of depression in the 1740s, due to competition from manufacturers of weaving towns in the North of England who, taking advantage of cheaper labour, began to make imitation Bocking bays, the local merchants and weavers were at last enjoying prosperity. Daniel Defoe, although he did not actually set foot in the town on his celebrated tour of England in the years 1719–24, described it from a distance as having become 'rich and populous' through the bay trade. The local master clothiers, meticulous about the quality of the cloth they produced, which had the reputation of being finer in texture than any woven elsewhere, were doing very well indeed. Bocking bays and says were especially sought after in Spain and Portugal.

Spinning was mostly done in the cottages by women and quite young children. The Savill business alone at this time employed over a thousand workers, and there were many other successful clothiers who deserve mention, including members of the Boosey, Nottidge, English, Maysent, Ruggles, Aylett and Tabor families. The name of Robert Maysent has gone down into history as manufacturer of the first 'long Bay'—or what today we should call a 'double-width' cloth.

A number of the Bocking clothiers are commemorated in the church, and many of them handsomely endowed the local charities. John Aylett, who died in February 1707 and was buried in the chancel under a slab of black marble, left three acres of land to be administered by a body of trustees drawn from the principal inhabitants of Bocking and Braintree, who were to serve the rents and 'equally divide the same between the said Parishes and then lay the same out for Linnen Cloth, to be given and distributed out for Shirts and Shifts to the most indigent persons of their several Parishes of honest life and conversation upon the 5th day of November yearly and every year for ever'.[54] This charity and several others providing bread or money or other necessities for the deserving poor have now been brought under one trust which is administered by the Church Commissioners.

The Maysent tomb at the eastern end of the south aisle has exceptionally beautiful wrought-iron railings. Erected by John Maysent of Bocking Hall in about 1723, in memory of his son John and daughter-in-law Judith, with their seven young children, it is in fact empty. No one has ever solved this mystery, but one theory is that John Maysent the elder died shortly after making arrangements for the construction of the vault and before he could carry out his intention of gathering into it from the churchyard the various family coffins. There may be a more gruesome explanation: during the Napoleonic Wars there was an acute shortage of metal for ammunition, and lead coffins were not infrequently requisitioned surreptitiously for this purpose. If this is what happened here, at least the elder Maysent was spared the knowledge of the fate of the pathetic little coffins of Judith (aged three years), Elizabeth (two years), John (one Year), Joseph (eight months), Rebecca (three years) and Mary (eight years) and those of their parents. In his will Maysent charged the property which was then the *Queen's Head* inn in Bradford Street with 40s. per annum for the maintenance of the family burial place, the surplus to be distributed by his heirs among the poor of the parish. Eventually this inn became a private dwelling, Maysent House.

The earlier John Maysent whose will,[55] dated 1695, is reproduced in part in Fig. 7, p. 89, was also a Bocking clothier, and it is of interest that after making the usual monetary bequests to his family he lists the equipment which he leaves to his son Jeremiah, which includes 'handles beams & skales waights basketts oyle kettles & tenters . . .'. A tenter was a wooden framework on which the milled cloth was stretched to dry, usually in the fields, and from it is derived the expression 'to be on tenterhooks', meaning in an anxious or uneasy position.

Several old Bocking inns such as *The Woolpack* (now 77–83 Bradford Street) were later converted into private residences, and in some of them the original carved beams have been preserved. In their heyday these elegant Church Lane and Bradford Street properties belonged to the wealthy bay weavers. They were the hub of 18th-century Bocking society: Wentworth House, with its lovely Queen Anne Porch; Tabor House, in Church Lane, which has a picturesque overhang, a lovely moulded beam over the entrance and a very fine set of chimney stacks. Others once worth a mention are today in a sorry state of disrepair.

It was customary throughout the 18th century for young boys (and occasionally girls) to be apprenticed to a trade. From nearly 300 'Apprenticeship Indentures' made at Bocking between the years 1704 and 1796 which have been preserved,[56] it appears that 11 out of every 12 apprentices in the town entered the cloth trade. Of these, about 80 per cent. were apprenticed to bay weavers, wool combers or fullers. Thus Samuel Ellen, on 7 June 1736, entered into an agreement with William Windle, bay weaver, for a period of 10 years. During this time he promised to serve his Master faithfully, to keep his secrets and his 'lawful commandments every where gladly do'. He was not to haunt taverns, inns or alehouses, nor was he to play at cards, dice or any unlawful games. The indenture in fact lays down the standard code of behaviour: 'He shall not matrimony contract nor fornication commit nor from the service of his said Master Day or Night shall absent himself; but in all Things, as an honest and faithful Apprentice, shall and will demean and behave himself toward his said Master and all his during the said Term'. The master, for his part, contracted to teach the young lad the 'Art or Mystery of Bay Weaving, . . . finding and allowing unto his said Apprentice sufficient Meat, Drink, Washing, Lodging and all other Necessaries' and at the end of the term he was to give him 'two Suits of Cloths, that is to say, One good new Suit of all things for Holy Days and his working Cloths for working Days . . .'.

The cloth boom lasted until the year 1787. After that date Bocking was quite unable to compete with the large-scale manufacture of cheap cloth emanating from the north of England. A huge market for this inferior quality cloth was created by the outbreak of the Revolution in France, when all woollen manufacture in that country ceased and the French Army turned to Britain to supply material for uniforms. During the Napoleonic Wars the export of Bocking bays to Spain and Portugal was halted, and by the time hostilities ended in 1815 the people living in those countries had accustomed themselves to lighter fabrics more suited to the climate.

This collapse of the market for Bocking cloth meant disaster to many of the local firms. And this time the depression was permanent. In August 1793 a house-to-house survey of the town and parish showed a total of 2,943 inhabitants.⁵⁷ By 1801 the population had decreased to 2,680 and was to sink lower. By 1804 all the master clothiers except John Savill had gone out of business. In the words of the author of *Journal of a Very Young Lady's Tour from Canonbury to Aldborough,* published (in rhyme) in 1804:

> We saw two large townships called Braintree and Bocking,
> Where the tale of distress was of late years most shocking.

John Savill, last in the line of the great Bocking clothiers, made a spirited attempt to revive the local trade by using water power instead of horses to turn his machinery. To this end, in January 1813 he bought the old water mill in Bocking Church Street, on the river Blackwater. The enterprise was not a success, and six-and-a-half years later he had to admit failure. By that time a small silk manufacturing trade was growing up in the district, pioneered first by a man called Newman and then by George Courtauld, who in 1810 had opened a silk factory at Braintree. Savill's private diary for 4 September 1819⁵⁸ records the sale to Samuel Courtauld (son of George) of what the Courtauld's historian, C. H. Ward-Jackson, later called 'one of the last baize mills in Essex'. When Courtauld was subsequently unable to proceed with the purchase, Savill agreed to lease the mill to him for a period of 14 years with an option to purchase. On Savill's death in 1828, Courtauld exercised his option and established a factory at Bocking. During the lean years of the early 19th century he gave employment to hundreds of local people, which helped to arrest the decline of prosperity and population. By 1831 the town's population had risen again to 3,128.

The production of silk at Bocking was to continue for about a hundred years, and also that of an embossed crape which became known in the trade as 'crape anglais'. There was a great demand at this period for black mourning crape, and the quality of Bocking crape was acknowledged to be the best on the market. The fabric was woven at factories in Halstead and Earls Colne, but brought to Bocking to be 'finished'. The secret finishing process was so closely guarded that each workman was sworn before a magistrate not to divulge it, and the machines were kept locked when not in use.

Fashions change with the years, however, and from about 1885 the crape trade went into a sharp decline. It was said that the Princess of Wales, later Queen Alexandra, with her strongly-voiced dislike of the fabric, was largely to blame; when Edward VII died in 1910 she ordered no crape for Court mourning. Nevertheless, Bocking continued to produce crape for export to France until the German occupation of that country in 1940. The silk trade also was faced with difficulties, and following the removal of duty on imported silks in 1860, the firm was unable to compete with foreign manufactures.

It was not until towards the end of the century, after the death of Samuel Courtauld, that the firm was reorganised. This marked the end of the old cottage weaving industry. The various processes were segregated, and the Bocking factory began to specialise in dyeing and finishing, in a new three-storey building on the site of the Savill water mill. Many Bockonians find employment there today, and the town is proud of its long association with the vast concern which has developed from a small family silk business through artificial silks into the synthetic fabrics for which Courtaulds are now renowned the world over.

Aristocrats and a Royal Guest

Paradoxically, as the local cloth trade went into decline, Bocking Deanery was to open its doors to its most eminent occupant yet—a Duke's son and a man who had already risen in the Church to the rank of Bishop. But we are moving too fast; 25 years before that another Dean, Nicholas Wakeham, held the office.

Dr. Wakeham arrived in Bocking in November 1774. He came from a sporting family of West-country farmers whose crest was a white greyhound with black spots, resembling—as the late Mr. Alfred Hills put it—'an athletic Dalmation'. His coat of arms bore three hunting horns, which was thought to be some kind of pun on 'wake 'em'. He had been Captain of the School at Eton and a Fellow of King's College, Cambridge. Whether he brought a wife or family to Bocking is not known, but he had three sons, all of whom entered the Church.

Evidently Dr. Wakeham found some of the Deanery property in a sad state, for on 17 July 1775 he sent a petition to the

Archbishop of Canterbury asking that 'an old Farm House containing Thirty Feet in length and about Nineteen Feet in breadth, Also the remains of an old Barn the Dimensions of which cannot well be ascertained', which were in his possession as Rector of Bocking and which had 'become so ruinous as not to be worth repairing', might be taken down. This petition has been preserved in Lambeth Palace Library, together with the deed signed by Archbishop Cornwallis appointing a commission to view the buildings in question and the commission's report, dated 24 July, which is endorsed, 'Let a Faculty be Granted. Fred. Cant'.

The Dean left no personal record of his office, but the accounts for the Deanery during his term at Bocking are also at Lambeth. Wakeman must have been highly esteemed in the Church, for in 1801 he was chosen as Bishop-elect of Lichfield. He was then in his seventies. He died on Christmas Day the same year, still Dean of Bocking, and was buried in the chancel of St. Mary's Church.

In 1802 the Bishop of St. Davids, Lord George Murray, second son of the 3rd Duke of Atholl, was appointed to the Deanery. It is unlikely, however, that he was much seen in the parish, as he fulfilled many duties elsewhere; his term of office was also one of the shortest. He died at Cavendish Square, London, on 3 June 1803 as a result of a severe chill caught while waiting for his carriage outside the House of Lords. Three weeks later his youngest brother, Lord Charles Murray-Aynsley, succeeded him at Bocking.

Lord Charles had married in June 1793 Alicia Aynsley, a member of the Mitford family; she had adoped that surname on inheriting a large fortune from her great-uncle, Gawen Aynsley. The couple had met and fallen in love at the house of her guardian, Dr. George Mitford of Morpeth, Northumberland. Years later, Mary Russell Mitford, who was Alicia's cousin, wrote a most entertaining account of the happy pair at the time of their betrothal:

How the first step in the business, the inevitable and awful ceremonial of a declaration of love and a proposal of marriage, was ever brought about, has always been to

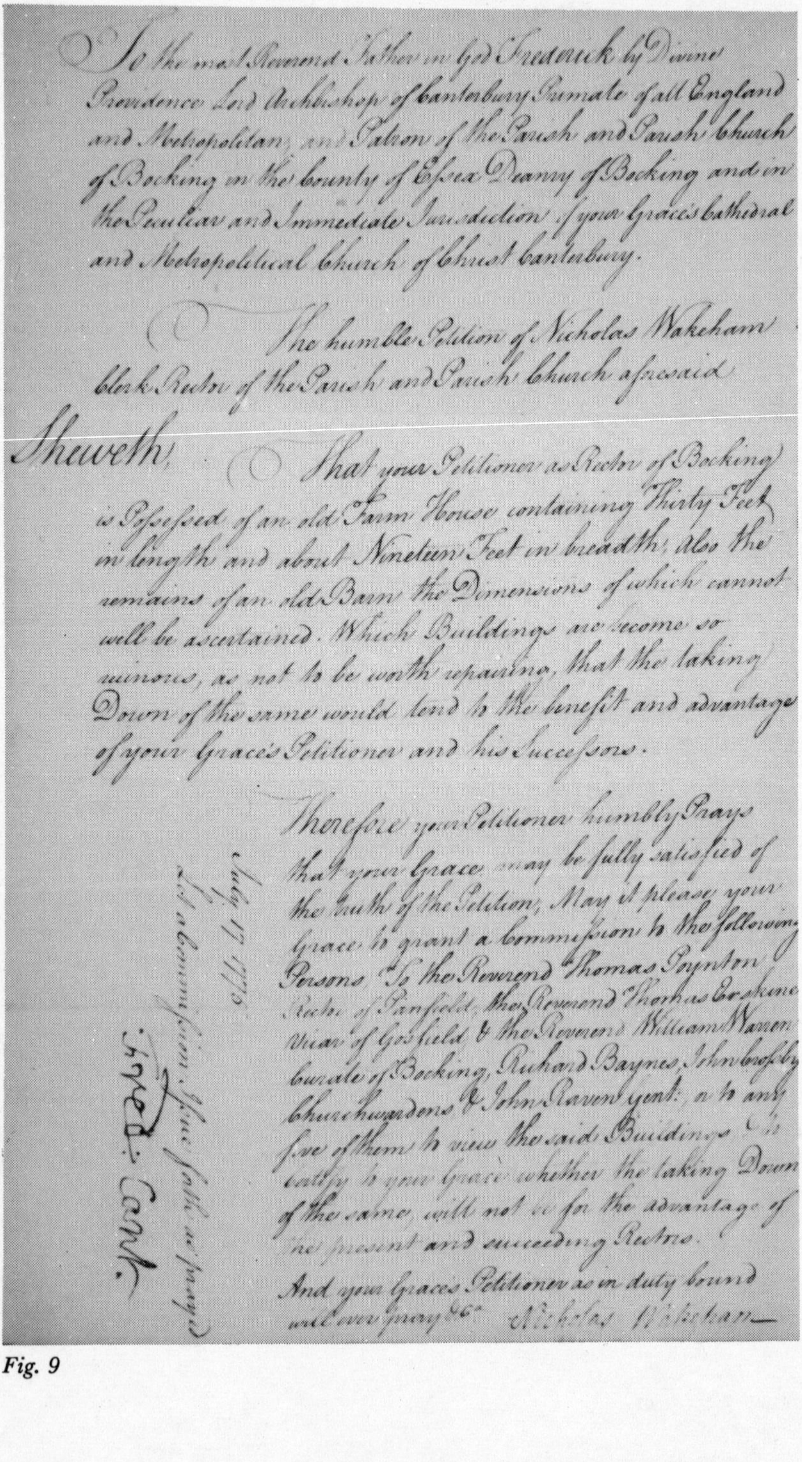
To the most Reverend Father in God Frederick by Divine Providence Lord Archbishop of Canterbury Primate of all England and Metropolitan, and Patron of the Parish and Parish Church of Bocking in the County of Essex Deanry of Bocking and in the Peculiar and Immediate Jurisdiction of your Grace's Cathedral and Metropolitical Church of Christ Canterbury.

The humble Petition of Nicholas Wakeham Clerk Rector of the Parish and Parish Church aforesaid

Sheweth, That your Petitioner as Rector of Bocking is Possessed of an old Farm House containing Thirty Feet in length and about Nineteen Feet in breadth; also the remains of an old Barn the Dimensions of which cannot well be ascertained. Which Buildings are become so ruinous, as not to be worth repairing, that the taking Down of the same would tend to the benefit and advantage of your Grace's Petitioner and his Successors.

Therefore your Petitioner humbly Prays that your Grace may be fully satisfied of the truth of the Petition, May it please your Grace to grant a Commission to the following Persons, To the Reverend Thomas Poynton Rector of Panfield, the Reverend Thomas Erskine Vicar of Gosfield, & the Reverend William Warren Curate of Bocking, Richard Baynes, John Crosby Churchwardens & John Raven Gent. or to any five of them to view the said Buildings & to certify to your Grace whether the taking Down of the same, will not be for the advantage of the present and succeeding Rectors.

And your Graces Petitioner as in duty bound will ever pray &c. Nicholas Wakeham—

July 17 1770
Let a Commission issue forth as prayed
Fred: Cant.

Fig. 9

Fees due to the Principal Registers of the
Deanry of Bocking in the County of Essex, from
the 30th December 1775 to the 30th Sept.r 1776.

1776

Feb.y 8th. By Probate   Robert Reymer   .. 2.. 6
                      Registring 1/   .. 1.. 8

March 1st By Ditto   Samuel May   .. 2.. 6
                      Registring 3/6   .. 2.. 4

April 9th By Ditto   John Bragg   .. 2.. 6
                      Registring 2/6   1.. 8

    By Ditto   Oliver Johnson   .. 2.. 6
                      Registring 2/6   .. 1.. 8

May 21st By Admon   John Reymer   .. 0.. 8

June 1st By Probate   Mary Colman   .. 2.. 6
                      Registring 4/   .. 2.. 8

    18 By Admon   Elizabeth Lovell   .. 0.. 8

    By Presentments of nine Parishes 1776   .. 15.. ..

    By one Licence passed by the Rev.d Mr Richards after the
    death of Dr Hall & before Dr Wakeham's appointm.t   } .. 4.. ..
    omitted in last Account

    By 5 Licences passed by Dr Wakeham to the   } 1. 0.. 0
    Visitation 27th May 1776

    By 7 Licences passed by the Rev.d Mr Richards   } 1.. 8.. ..
    to Visitation 27th May 1776

Augst 2nd By Admon   Elizabeth Crosby   .. 0.. 8

Oct 1st By Probate   George Frost   .. 2.. 6
   (Mr Johnson Ex.r Sq.r)   Registring 7/6   .. 5.. ..

    By 3 Licences passed by Dr Wakeham from Visitation } .. 12.. ..
    1776 to the 30 Sep.t following

    By 2 Licences passed by Rev.d Mr Richards from } .. 8.. ..
    last Visitation 1776 to S.r 30 Sep.t following

                                   £7. 0. 0

Fig. 10

me one of the most unsolvable of mysteries—an enigma without the word.

Lord Charles, as fine a young man as one should see in a summer's day, tall, well made, with handsome features, fair capacity, excellent education, and charming temper, had an infirmity which went nigh to render all these good gifts of no avail: a shyness, a bashfulness, a timidity most painful to himself and distressful to all about him . . . I myself, a child not five years old, one day threw him into an agony of blushing, by running up to his chair in mistake for my papa. Now I was a shy child, a very shy child, and as soon as I arrived in front of His Lordship, and found that I had been misled by a resemblance of dress, by the blue coat and buff waistcoat, I first of all crept under the table, and then flew to hide my face in my mother's lap; my poor fellow-sufferer, too big for one place of refuge, too old for the other, had nothing for it but to run away, which, the door being luckily open, he happily accomplished.

That a man of such a temperament, who could hardly summon up courage to say 'How d'ye do?' should ever have wrought himself up to the point of putting the great question, was wonderful enough; but that he should have submitted himself to undergo the ordeal of what was called in those days a public wedding, was more wonderful still.

Perhaps the very different temper of the lady may offer some solution to the last of these riddles; perhaps (I say it in all honour, for there is no shame in offering some encouragement to a bashful suitor) it may assist us in expounding them both.

Of a certainty, my fair cousin was pre-eminently gifted with those very qualities in which her lover was deficient. Everything about her was prompt and bright, cheerful and self-possessed. Nearly as tall as himself, and quite as handsome, it was of the beauty what is called showy—a showy figure, a showy complexion. We felt at a glance that those radiant, well-opened hazel eyes, had never quailed before mortal glance, and that that clear round cheek, red and white like a dairy, had never been guilty

of a blush in the whole of its life . . . she would not
have minded a coronation; on the contrary, she would
have been enchanted to have been a queen regnant; but,
as a coronation was out of the question, she had no
objection, taking publicity as part of the happiness, to
a wedding as grand as the resources of a country town
could make it . . .[59]

The marriage took place on 18 June 1793, and little Mary
Russell Mitford, aged five, was a bridesmaid. A large company
of relatives on both sides of the family attended, and the
wedding procession stretched for nearly half a mile. The
bridegroom by Royal licence added his wife's surname to his
own and was known thereafter as Lord Charles Murray-Aynsley
(or sometimes as Lord Charles Aynsley). Their seat was Little
Harle Tower in Northumberland, which had been Lady Charles's
inheritance.

The Murray-Aynsleys had nine children, four of whom died in
infancy. At the time the family took up residence at the Deanery,
in the summer of 1803, there were in the nursery three small
girls, Charlotte, Atholl Keturah and Elizabeth Anne, and one
boy, John. Another son, Charles Edward, would be born at
Bocking in 1805.

The Dukes of Atholl had for generations been Lords of the
Isle of Man, and although the sovereignty of that island had
been purchased by the British Crown in 1765, the family still
retained manorial rights and the patronage of the See. These
rights were acquired by Parliament in 1828, but not before they
had earned one of the Murray-Aynsley daughters, Atholl, the
unofficial title of 'the last Princess of Man'.

During the Murray-Aynsleys' time at Bocking the exiled
French King Louis XVIII came to live at nearby Gosfield Hall,
a mansion lent to him by the Marquess of Buckingham. There
are many stories of his stay: of the mimic court held there in
the Bourbon tradition; of the King dining in public, in accordance
with old French custom, when the inhabitants of the neighbourhood were allowed to pass through the dining room in procession
to witness the spectacle. There was one old Essex woman who
remembered meeting the King and his attendants when out
walking near the Hall as a child. Louis noticed her and wished

to give her something, but his pockets proved to be empty and
the best that one member of his retinue could produce was a
halfpenny. 'I ought to have kept that halfpenny', the old lady
used to tell her grandchildren years later.

So far as Bocking is concerned, the event of the century
took place on the night of 18 February 1808, when the French
King and his court attended a dinner given in his honour by Lord
and Lady Charles Murray-Aynsley at the Deanery. Mary Russell
Mitford, who received a letter from her cousin, 'Lady C.',
immediately afterwards describing the occasion, lost no time in
reporting every detail to her husband:

> . . . Her ladyship has been in a very grand bustle, as the
> King of France, Monsieur the Comte d'Artois, the Duke
> d'Angoulême, Duke de Berry, Duke de Grammont and
> the Prince de Condé, with all the nobles that composed
> His Majesty's suite at Gosfield, dined at the Deanery
> last Thursday. Mr. and Mrs. Pepper, Lady Fitzgerald's
> daughter, were asked to meet him, because she was brought
> up and educated in the French Court in Louis XVI's reign;
> General and Mrs. Milner for the same reason, and Colonel,
> Mrs. and Miss Burgoyne—all the party quick at languages.
>
> The snow storms alarmed Lady C. not a little, for it
> prevented the carrier going to town in the first instance,
> and in the second she began to fear the King might not
> be able to come, after all the preparations made for him.
> The Milners were so anxious about it that the General who
> commands at Colchester, ordered five hundred pioneers
> to clear the road from that city to Bocking. On His
> Majesty's approach the Bocking bells proclaimed it, and
> on driving up, the full military band which Lord C. had
> engaged for the occasion struck up 'God Save the King'
> in the entrance passage. In His Majesty's coach were
> Monsieur the Comte d'Artois and the Dukes d'Angoulême
> and Berry. They arrived a little before five o'clock, and
> Lady Charles handed His Majesty from his carriage into the
> drawing-room, and introduced the illustrious guest to those
> friends who were invited upon this interesting occasion. His
> Majesty in the most affable and engaging manner entered into
> conversation with every individual present.

All stood till dinner was announced, when our cousin handed His Majesty—Lord C. walking before him with a candle. The King sat at the top of the table with Lady C. on his right and Lord C. on his left. Mrs. Milner's and Mrs. Pepper's French butlers were lent for the occasion. The bill of fare was in French, and the King appeared well pleased with his entertainment. The French nobility, who compose His Majesty's suite, were in full dress and wore the insignia of their respective orders.

The company were three hours at dinner, and at eight the dessert was placed on the table—claret and all kinds of French wine, fruit, etc., a beautiful cake at the top with 'Vive le Roi de France' baked round it, and the quarterings of the French army in coloured pastry, which had a novel and pretty effect. The three youngest children then entered with white satin military sashes over their shoulders upon which were painted in bronze 'Vive le Roi de France—Prospérité à Louis dix-huit'. Charles, on being asked for a toast, immediately gave 'The King of France', which was drunk with the utmost sensibility by all present, and one of the little girls came up to His Majesty and, with great expression, spoke the lines in French, composed for the occasion.

Louis soon followed the ladies into the drawing-room, when again all stood, and Lady C. served her Royal guest with coffee, which being over, she told him that some of the neighbouring families were coming for a little dance in the dining-room and that perhaps His Majesty would be seated at cards. He good humouredly said he would first go and pay his respects in the next room, which was the thing she wished; therefore handed him in, his family and nobles following, which was a fine sight for those assembled, in all sixty-two. At the King's desire she introduced each person to him by name, and, on the King's sitting down, the band struck up, and Monsieur, who is supposed to be the finest dancer in Europe, led off with Lady C., who, in spite of Lord Charles's horror and her own fears for her lame ankle, hopped down two country dances with him, and they were followed by Charlotte and the Duke d'Angoulême . . .[60]

What hostess would not have sympathised with the anxiety
of Lady Charles on that great day? Would all the delicacies she
had ordered from London to tempt the Royal palate arrive in
time? The exceptionally heavy snowfall had practically cut off all
communication with the metropolis, and the carrier who plied
daily between *The Woolpack* inn and London was unable to
get through. To the astonishment of the local inhabitants, a
contingent of General Milner's soldiers arrived and began to
clear a road. Later that afternoon, almost every Bockonian
braved the cold to witness the Royal procession, the carriage
wheels crunching on the frozen roads, the French courtiers in
ceremonial attire, all going past to the accompaniment of the
Bocking bells.

Three months later the Dean was dead. He was only thirty-six.
Bishop-elect of London, Lord Charles was on his way from
Bocking to take up his new duties. Travelling by coach, he
stopped overnight at the *Black Lion,* Bishop's Stortford, where
he caught a sudden chill and died on 5 May. He was taken back
to Bocking for burial.

After the funeral, the widow with her five surviving children
decided to stay on at Bocking, although of course she had to
move out of the Deanery to make way for the new incumbent.
Whether this move was forced on her too quickly, whether
there was some 'awkwardness' over the financial arrangements,
or whether it was simply that the new people at the Deanery
were not 'grand' enough for Lady Charles, we do not know,
but a definite coolness seems to have persisted for some time
between the two families. Perhaps the root of the trouble was
that Lady Charles resented another woman stepping into her
rôle as lady of the manor. She must also have found that she
could no longer afford to live in the style to which she had been
accustomed—though what had become of her inherited fortune
remains a mystery. Undoubtedly the Murray-Aynsleys had lived
at the Deanery in extravagant style, in the tradition of some
of their predecessors; the lavish entertainment of Royal and
other guests must have made a sizeable inroad into their private
resources. At any rate, the money had been used up, for the
Mitford family are said to have been called on to help their
cousin financially at this time. But not for very long. Lady
Charles had never been robust and, after months of suffering

from some incurable disease, she died at Bocking in June 1813 and was buried beside her husband in the Aynsley vault there.

Twenty years later, when their daughter Atholl returned to Bocking as the wife of another Dean, Sir Herbert Oakeley, she commissioned a memorial tablet to be placed above their tomb. It was inscribed: 'A daughter's affection for parents prematurely lost'. Atholl had been only seven years old when she lost her father, and not quite 12 when her mother died.

The Wordsworths

The Dean who followed Lord Charles was Christopher Wordsworth, younger brother of the poet. Whatever it was that he and his wife had been guilty of doing, or of not doing, to Lady Charles Murray-Aynsley, the injury rankled: nearly 18 months after their arrival at Bocking the former Dean's widow was still referring to the newcomers in the most scathing terms. She wrote to her eldest daughter, Charlotte, from Bocking on 27 October 1809:

> When I tell you, my darling Girl, that *I* celebrated the National Jubilee [of George III], you will not be surprised to hear that I have suffered dreadfully from the exertion I made.
>
> Sunday I walked to Church and as Charles [her youngest son, then aged four] and myself got to the Deanery gate, Mr. and Mrs. Wordsworth were walking towards it. Charles stopped and screamed out 'Oh my Papa, my own Dear Papa!'—and was running towards the Gate when I got hold of him and said it was Mr. Wordsworth. He trembled from head to foot, and afterwards told me it was the dress which struck him, Mr. Wordsworth being in Gown and Cassock.
>
> Sunday the Miss Nottidges called and said their aged parents were to be at the Ball and supper to drink the King's health. 'Then so will I too' was the reply. Finding the Deanery family were to be there had no effect on me; I had never met with them, & entertained too great a share of contempt for their conduct towards me to

make me in the least uncomfortable to see them; besides,
as my intention of going to the supper flew quick, I did
not expect they would put themselves in my way. Tuesday
brought me a letter from the Stewards saying that in the
name of the Parish they were to express their deep sense
of the compliment I intended to pay them and beg
permission to call upon me at any hour I would appoint,
to escort me to the White Hart, for which purpose they
would leave the Ballroom. I answered—I should be very
happy to shew my attachment to the inhabitants of
Bocking, & loyalty to my King and as supper was to be
at eleven I would enter the Ballroom at a quarter of an
hour before it; but begged the Stewards not to come
for me.

Wednesday morning at one all the singers came with
their Church instruments, & played the Coronation Anthem
at my door; at three the military band came & played
'God save the King' . . .

[On Thursday] We reached Church at half past ten.
In justice to the truth I must say a better discourse than
Mr. Wordsworth's was never preached from any pulpit.
He has a full tone and excellent delivery. His language is
impressive, and his words well chosen and put together . . .
In the evening I was waited upon by our poor Parishioners,
who wished to show their regard by taking me to the
White Hart without horses, but this I refused. At
seven the Crown in coloured lamps with a garland of
flowers was placed upon the garden door, and green
baize laid from the front doorstep to it which was then
opened, and from the street it looked beautiful. The
crowd was soon immense, and the carriages stopped to
look at it on their way to the Assembly Room. It struck
me that the Servants were the only class that were over-
looked in the general joy; for the hearts of the Poor were
made to laugh, and the Rich had sumptuous repasts, but
servants were to drag on with their daily labour unheeded
and unregarded. I therefore desired mine to ask all those
they knew to a dance and supper; and thirty arrived, with
medals and devices and at eleven sat down to a plentiful
supper, of beef and 'plumb' pudding, with music, strong

beer and punch. A little before this the pony carriage drove up, and on getting in I observed about forty of our Parishioners with Flambeaux who ranged themselves on each side to light me to the White Hart. Your sisters and Mr. White with me. Before the carriage stopped, the crowd became immense, and the acclamations rent the air, with every joy to see me again out, and blessings on us all. I trembled from head to foot; all my borrowed determination to do my duty forsook me, and for some time I felt totally unable to leave the carriage; the Stewards however having come down to receive me and the anxious looks of my sweet little girls aroused me, and I was led up the room with the most marked attention.

Mrs. Wordsworth got a headache and could not go. But Mr. Wordsworth enquired what all that noise and sudden commotion meant—he was told it must be for Lady Charles, on which he retired into one of the ante rooms, took a French leave, walked to the Deanery and was no more seen . . . As soon as the King's health was drunk, we returned home . . .[61]

Quite plainly Lady Charles revelled in being the centre of attention!

With the Wordsworths in residence the Deanery was once more a family home. Four years earlier Dr. Wordsworth had married the daughter of a Birmingham Quaker, Priscilla Lloyd. She was the eldest sister of the poet Charles Lloyd, a friend whom Christopher Wordsworth had made at Cambridge and a member of the Lamb-Coleridge-Wordsworth circle. She had already borne him three sons, John, Charles, and Christopher; three more babies, only one a girl, were to be born at Bocking, but did not survive.

Born in 1774 at Cockermouth and a pupil at Hawkshead Grammar School, Christopher Wordsworth had gone up to Cambridge as a pensioner in 1792. There he had soon achieved academic distinction, graduating as 10th wrangler in 1796 and being elected a Fellow of Trinity College two years later. He took his M.A. in 1799 and became a Doctor of Divinity in 1810. In the meantime an appointment as private tutor to Charles Manners-Sutton, a son of the Bishop of Norwich,

secured for him very early on two most influential patrons.
In 1804 the Bishop presented Wordsworth to the Rectory of
Ashby with Oby and Thinne in Norfolk. This enabled him to
marry. The following year, when the elder Manners-Sutton
became Archbishop of Canterbury, he made Wordsworth his
domestic chaplain; later, in 1806, transferring him to the
Rectory at Woodchurch in Kent and in 1808 to Bocking.

As soon as Dr. and Mrs. Wordsworth settled in at the
Deanery, it became clear that sumptuous entertainment and
high living were now of the past. The new Dean had too many
childhood memories of poverty (he and his brother William
owed their education almost entirely to the generosity of two
uncles), and he had learned at an early age the wisdom of
thrift. Not only that, he was a man of simple tastes, high
principles and industry— especially the latter. The poet, in
an early letter about his brother's career, wrote somewhat
enviously: 'That same industry is an old Roman quality, and
nothing is to be done without it'. Some people thought him
pompous and priggish, but Henry Crabb Robinson, the diarist,
on meeting the Dean and his wife for the first time, noted:

> She pleases me, and so does he, tho' he has all the
> elements of a high priest in him, tempered by domestic
> virtues . . . They did not appear to have heard lately from
> the poet, and the want of intimacy there ought to subsist
> between the brothers is the only unfavourable trait in the
> Doctor's character or circumstances . . .[62]

Many years later, the Dean's son Charles recalled his father's
habit of strolling about the fields on Saturday mornings speaking
his prepared Sunday sermon to the winds and hedges. Although
he was no longer at Bocking then, but at Buxted in Sussex,
where he spent the last years of his life, it seems likely that he
adopted this custom quite early and may often have been
seen striding through the Essex countryside or through the
Deanery grounds similarly engaged.

Certainly Dr. Wordsworth took himself and his duties most
seriously, and Bocking respected him for it. He might have done
more had it not been for his commitments in London, where he
was frequently required to be in attendance on Archbishop

Manners-Sutton. Priscilla Wordsworth's letters to her father, written from the Deanery, contain many references to her husband's absence at Lambeth, while she is preoccupied at home with her three boys. Thus, on 7 August 1815:

> . . . Wordsworth got through his day at Lambeth I imagine with great credit, though I never get from him any account of himself, or the commendation he receives. 'Decently', or 'tolerably', are generally the highest epithets he bestows on his own doings, so that if I get such expressions as these I interpret them accordingly. He is now engaged on two more public occasions in London—one for the London National Schools, and the other for Hackney, so that there is no danger of his talents rusting for want of exercise . . .[63]

Provision of education for the poor had interested the Dean for a number of years, and in 1811 he had been a co-founder, together with his friend, the London wine merchant and philanthropist, Joshua Watson, of the National Society.

In spite of his many other concerns, the welfare of the poor in his own parish did not escape the Dean's attention. He was a most methodical man, and there is in existence a brown leather-covered notebook[64] in which, in the neatest of handwritings, he carefully listed the different charities endowed at Bocking over the years. These began with the almshouse, or *Maison de Dieu*, built by John Doreward in 1440 and enlarged through the generosity of Sergeant William Bendlowes of Wethersfield, who by a deed dated 4 July 1571 provided funds in perpetuity from his estates at Great Bardfield for distribution to the inmates and for the repair and upkeep of the almshouses. It ended with several 18th-century bequests such as that under the Will of John Aylett, 1707, which directed that after his wife's death the profits from his estate should be divided between the parishes of Bocking and Braintree 'for Linnen Cloth to be given and distributed out for shirts and shifts'. After Dean Wordsworth's time another charity was added to his list, that of Mr. Polley, who left £10 per annum for the distribution of bread to the most deserving and necessitous.

One of the older-established charities was that of John Gauden for the establishment of a school and maintenance of a schoolmaster 'for the teaching of thirty poor Boys to read English and to write . . .'. In Gauden's day the parish had of course been nowhere near the size it was in the early 1800s, and Wordsworth felt very strongly that it was not right to deprive other poor children of educational opportunity, nor that such a limitation would have been Gauden's intention. He therefore persuaded his fellow trustees of the need for enlarged premises and he recorded with some satisfaction in his notebook that 'subscriptions and benefactions were solicited' for the building of a new schoolroom for boys, for further improvements of the existing school and for the establishment and support of a school for girls. He further adds that the new boys' school was opened officially on 18 November 1811 and that for the girls in a room at the workhouse (at the bottom of Deanery Hill) on 26 October 1812. The school was financed by a trust whose income derived from money and arable lands given by local donors. Dr. Wordsworth was the prime mover and first chairman, and later Deans automatically took the Chair. (At the beginning of this century, however, owing to lack of provision for the appointment of new trustees following the death of previous trustees, it was for a short time administered by the Chelmsford Diocesan Board. It is now under the control of the Department of Education and Science.)

There had been a friendly rivalry between the towns of Bocking and Braintree since the 17th century. Now that Bocking had a new school it is likely that the Braintree lads revived an old rhyme mocking those of neighbouring districts:

> Braintree boys, brave boys,
> Bocking boys, rats.
> Church Street, puppy dogs,
> High Garrett, cats.[65]

The Wordsworths were happy at Bocking, and the Dean, when offered the Bishopric of Calcutta in 1814, declined to uproot the family from their rural English life. Priscilla too came to love the Deanery and the grounds. 'We have the music of the groves here in great perfection', she wrote

to her mother in June 1812. 'I long for someone to share in
the fresh beauties that are blooming around me, for it they
cannot inspire gladness, at least they fill the heart with peace
and thankfulness.'[66] The Dean was on one of his visits to
Lambeth at the time. By this date all three boys attended
daily at the Bocking Academy in Bradford Street, known
locally as 'Hagon's', and later 'Saltmarsh's', from the name of
the schoolmaster.

The young girl with the bright complexion and fine brown
eyes who at the age of 16 had begun to see beyond the
Quaker environment in which she had been brought up, had
developed into a woman of exceptional character. She had
been baptised into the Anglican Church on her 23rd birthday,
the day of her marriage to Christopher Wordsworth. Parish
duties, domesticity and childbirth had filled her days ever
since, and her letters from Bocking are full of the progress
of young John, Charles and the baby 'Christy'. She set great
score by academic success, and had she known that of the
three sons, all of whom were to distinguish themselves in
university life, two would eventually become Bishops, it would
have made her very happy. She was not to know it, but she
was in fact the mother not only of a Bishop of St. Andrews
and a Bishop of Lincoln, but also the grandmother of a Bishop
of Salisbury, which was, as E. V. Lucas commented in *Charles
Lamb and the Lloyds,* 'no bad achievement for a Quaker's
daughter'. Unhappily, Priscilla was not to live to witness any
of her boys' successes, for in October 1815, at the age of only
34, she died giving birth to her sixth child, the only girl, who
did not survive.

She had been greatly loved and was much missed in the
parish. Forty years later, when her son Charles revisited Bocking
he was astonished and deeply moved to find fresh turf on his
mother's grave; he was told that it had been tended regularly
by the wife of the village carpenter all those years as a mark
of esteem and gratitude for Mrs. Wordsworth's good works
among the local people.

With his wife's premature death, the light went out of
Dr. Wordsworth's life. He was a changed man. There was no
sister or female relative to run the Deanery or to mother the boys,
and 'this', wrote Bishop Charles Wordsworth in later life, 'I

felt intensely throughout my early days; so that I was wont
to compare myself to fruit against a wall, ripened only upon
one side'.[67]

Bocking held too many poignant memories for the Dean,
and in the spring of the following year he prevailed upon his
patron to allow him to exchange the Rectory for those of
St. Mary's, Lambeth, and Sundridge in Kent. Then when his
former pupil, Charles Manners-Sutton, became Speaker of the
House of Commons in 1817; Wordsworth was appointed as his
chaplain. In 1820, on the recommendation of the Archbishop,
he was elected to the Mastership of Trinity College, Cambridge.
He then relinquished Lambeth and Sundridge, receiving in their
place the Rectory of Buxted in Sussex.

At Cambridge Dr. Wordsworth led a very secluded life and
made few friends. The discipline which he sought to impose
was considered too strict, and his insistence on their more
frequent attendance at chapel made him particularly unpopular
with the undergraduates. Nevertheless he was Vice-Chancellor of
the University in 1820-1 and again in 1826-7. His Mastership at
Trinity was not, however, generally regarded as a success, and in
1841 Wordsworth resigned and took up permanent residence at
Buxted, where he was to spend his last years. He died in February
1846 and was buried in Buxted churchyard.

By this time two other Deans had come and gone at Bocking,
and major alterations had been made to the Deanery house under
the supervision of an eminent London architect.

Pigeons and Temper

Of Dr. Charles Barton, who followed Christopher Wordsworth
as Rector and Dean of Bocking in 1816 and held office until
1834, there are no records, except that he came from Kent,
where he had been Vicar of Rainham, Rector of Pluckley, and
Rector of Halstead.

He must have maintained the tradition of keeping pigeons
in the Gauden dovecote, for it is said to have been a favourite
sport among the local lads on Sunday mornings, when the
Bartons were in church, to visit the Deanery and throw stones
at the birds. That the culprits were ever caught at this pastime
is doubtful, even if they mis-timed the Dean's return, for

Barton was getting on in years and was not at all active. He had married rather late in life the daughter of a vicar of Braintree, a much younger woman, and while at the Deanery a daughter was born. For years afterwards a story used to be circulated in the district that one day this child, while chatting to her father, had quite innocently let slip the information that her grandfather, anticipating that his son-in-law the aged Dean would not live much longer, had—as she put it—'bought a beautiful house in Braintree for Mother and me to go and live in when you go to Heaven'. The old gentleman was apparently so incensed that he is said (according to one version of the tale) to have cut his wife out of his will forthwith and (according to another) to have forced her, under the terms of his will, to live at least 50 miles away from Bocking for the rest of her life.

Barton's will, dated 17 November 1821, and a codicil dated 22 September 1832, are at the Public Record Office[68] and shed some light on how this story got around. Whereas large sums of money, £15,000 and £10,000 respectively, are left to the Dean's two sons (possibly from an earlier marriage, but this is not stated), his widow is to receive only £300 within a month of his death, the dividends from £3,000 and £500 out of the sale of his furniture 'that she may be enabled to furnish a house in some provincial town' where he wishes her to reside for the more convenient education of the children. She was also to have an allowance of £100 for each child under the age of nine and £150 for each child aged 9–21, out of their share of the residue of the estate, as well as linen, china, books and 'small articles of easy conveyance which she may select', and the use of his plate during her lifetime.

The settlement was not exactly generous, but it did not amount to cutting her out altogether. Furthermore, to give the Dean the benefit of the doubt, he made no stipulation that she should live any distance from Bocking, or in any particular town; he seems to have been concerned primarily with his children's educational welfare.

Perhaps Mrs. Barton had expected a richer inheritance and in her disappointment and vexation made some indiscreet comments which were exaggerated and embroidered as they were passed on from one local gossip to another. What is sad is that

Charles Barton should be remembered only for one unfounded act of temper. There are no grounds to substantiate that he did otherwise than serve his parish—and the Deanery—lovingly and well.

'The Proudest Dean that ever came to Bocking'

During Dean Barton's 18-year term of office little was done to the rambling old house by way of decoration or repair, and before the new incumbent with his wife and young family moved in some major restoration work was put in hand.

Sir Herbert Oakeley brought to the Deanery a wife who already had links with Bocking: Atholl Keturah, the second daughter of Lord Charles Murray-Aynsley. Her father had been made Dean of Bocking when she was a child of two, and Atholl had spent the next 10 years of her life in the parish, five of them at the Deanery, while her father was alive. After losing both parents by the age of 12, she had lived until her marriage at Blair Castle with her uncle and aunt, the Duke and Duchess of Atholl.

The Dean himself, whose father, Sir Charles Oakeley, the first Baronet, received his title for services to India, had been born in Madras during his father's Governorship of that state. He had returned to England with his parents in 1794 and was educated at Westminster and Christ Church, Oxford. His first appointment after taking holy orders was that of domestic chaplain to a future Archbishop of Canterbury, Dr. William Howley, then Bishop of London, with whom he formed a lifelong friendship. In 1822 Oakeley was appointed Vicar of Ealing, but did not take up residence there until after his marriage.

'. . . I think dearest Atholl's prospect of happiness is secured, for the character of Mr. Oakeley is everything one can desire', wrote Charlotte, Lady Oswald (Atholl's eldest sister) to Mary Russell Mitford on 31 March 1826. 'The accounts of Mr. Oakeley are charming; he is handsome, he is agreeable, he is good and amiable, he has quite enough of this world's goods, and ultimately he is very likely to be a Bishop . . .'[69]

They were married by the Bishop of London at St. Margaret's, Westminster, on 5 June 1826. Judging from their portraits, they made a striking couple: he rather dashing, with bold eyes and

unruly hair, she a fragile beauty. Three months later, the first
Baronet died and the title passed to his elder son, Charles. He
was to live for only three more years, however, and in June 1829,
there being no male issue, Herbert, as the next surviving brother,
succeeded to the baronetcy.

Both Herbert and Atholl were popular among their relations.
When the news was circulated that Dr. Howley had offered them
'one of the most desirable livings in his gift, the Deanery of
Bocking', a huge 'round robin' signed by members of the family
was sent to congratulate Lady Oakeley on her husband's appointment. Her aunt, the widowed Lady George Murray, herself once
the wife of a former Dean, wrote separately:

> Most sincerely do we congratulate Sir Herbert and you
> on the welcome intelligence which the note I received
> last night conveyed to us; it is one of those happy
> circumstances that falls to the lot of few to have so many
> agreeable circumstances connected with the appointment,
> for the recollection of former happy days I have no doubt
> will render you both particularly acceptable at Bocking,
> and I shall have very great pleasure in paying you a little
> visit there . . .[70]

Much needed to be done to the Deanery before they would
be able to think of entertaining guests. That Atholl, on her
first visit of inspection, recognised in the nursery the same
faded wallpaper that she had known in her own childhood, is
some measure of the state of the house. With three young
children between the ages of four and seven, and a new baby
born the previous November, not to mention the probability
of others to come—in the event, two more Oakeley children
were to be born at Bocking—they seriously considered complete
rebuilding.

The advice of a prominent London architect was sought:
Thomas Hopper (1776-1856), who had made a name for
himself enlarging and altering the mansions of Essex gentry.
He found that the roof·of the Deanery was sound, and the
idea of rebuilding was soon modified into one of major
reconstruction. This included the casing and cement rendering
of the entire building, the construction of a new brick service

wing and many 'refinements' to the interior such as pine panelling in several rooms, which unfortunately masked the original Tudor timbers and wall frescoes, now since uncovered again. Alterations were made first to the existing house, so that the family could move in, and the new wing added the following year—a workman thoughtfully carved the date '1835' on one of the roof timbers in the new part.

On arrival at Bocking the Oakeleys not only took over a house that was in a state of neglect, but a parish that needed considerable reorganisation. Energetically they set about this task. Sunday School teachers were appointed, arrangements made for a weekday service at High Garrett for those unable to walk the distance to church on Sundays, and every week after Morning Service six deserving elderly members of the congregation were entertained to dinner. Under Lady Oakeley's presidency, a group of ladies divided the straggling parish into districts for the purpose of regular visiting and the administration of relief to the poor. And once a year, in the summer, everyone —young and old—was invited to a garden party at the Deanery.

In spite of all their efforts, it seems that Sir Herbert was not particularly well liked by the Bockonians. They thought him a snob, perhaps because of his reputedly ostentatious habit of turning his back on any tradesman who called at the house. They called him 'the proudest Dean that ever came to Bocking', because he never let them forget his relationship, through his wife, with the aristocracy. Nevertheless, the Dean did a great deal for them, in the face of formidable difficulties. In his first year at Bocking he had to contend with a violent outbreak of cholera in the neighbourhood, and later with fierce and long-drawn-out opposition on the part of Nonconformists in the parish to the Church Rate, which resulted in many stormy, even at times disorderly, Vestry meetings. But none of this upset his unruffled disposition.

Meanwhile there were additions to the family: a daughter, Adelaide Helena, in September 1836, and a son, Edward Murray, in May 1840. The older children were thriving, especially Herbert, the second son, who was beginning to show exceptional musical talent. His parents had taken him to a service at Lichfield Cathedral in 1837, an event which he was in later life to recall as outstanding in his childhood memory. 'I took the gilt and white paint of the organ for ivory and gold, and good Mr. Spofforth—the hidden worker of miracles, who seemed to play two organs at once, and, for all one knew, blew the bellows also—for some saint or demigod.' It must have been awe-inspiring for a child of seven who had been used only to the village band which up to that time accompanied the church services at Bocking. The excursion was memorable, too, for an incident on the homeward journey when their carriage stopped at an inn in Cambridge for the Dean to alight and learn the news. It made a great impression upon the children when he returned bearing a black-edged newspaper that announced the death of the King and told them that a young Queen—Victoria—was now on the throne.

Lady Oakeley encouraged her musical son to play the pianoforte and taught him to write his compositions on paper. He wrote his first anthem at the age of nine. At about this date a fund was started to raise money to buy an organ for Bocking parish church. His mother wrote to Herbert at Brentwood School:

> . . . Papa thinks you got on very well and that you have good abilities. In music, you are already the first of little men, and that too without any study, but other things must be acquired with study. You will be glad to hear Lady Frankland Bupell has sent me six shillings for our Organ . . .[71]

The instrument was duly purchased and installed at St. Mary's Church, and in the school holidays young Herbert received his first organ lessons. On 26 March 1842 his eldest brother noted in his diary: 'Herby played on the organ in church; the people were all astonished'. It was not long before he was entrusted with all the music on any saint's day that fell in the school holidays. The future Professor of Music at Edinburgh University was shaping well.

The Dean was proud of Herbert, and indeed devoted to all his growing family; so much so that in 1842 when the Bishopric of Gibraltar was offered to him, he declined it, preferring not to be separated from his sons during their education. He had already the previous summer accepted the Archdeaconry of Colchester in addition to Bocking.

Music was not the only talent of the Oakeley family. The Dean himself was given to writing poetry, an art which he had practised since his university days. And his youngest brother, a frequent visitor to the Deanery, Canon Frederick Oakeley, had translated *Adeste Fideles* into the popular English version, 'O Come All Ye Faithful'. Lady Oakeley spent a good deal of her leisure time at the Deanery on a series of flower paintings and sketches of the house and garden.

In December 1841 Atholl developed an illness which was to last for a long time. At first it was believed that she had caught a germ on one of her visits to the poor. Unable to throw off a persistent cough, doctors advised her to convalesce at Hastings during the winter months. She was never really well again, but gradually became worse and after much suffering died at Hastings in January 1844.

Sir Herbert never recovered from this blow. His beloved Atholl was buried in the Aynsley vault at Bocking, where he had a memorial tablet placed close to that she had erected to her parents. On the back of her portrait hanging at the Deanery he wrote an inscription in Latin which a friend of the family translated as 'How small a thing is intercourse with the living compared with the memory of thee'. He made a brave effort to carry on with his normal duties, but the continual storms over the Church Rate and then the death of a favourite daughter in January 1845 were altogether too much for him. On 27 March that same year, while dining in London, he too passed away. He was buried at Bocking.

Sixty-one Years

By 1845 Bocking was one of only five Peculiars in England remaining under the jurisdiction of Canterbury. To this important living in April that year Archbishop Howley appointed a young man of 31, then Rector of Monks Eleigh in Suffolk. Henry Carrington was rumoured to have only one lung and was not expected to survive for more than a few years; as it turned out, he was to achieve the distinction of holding the office of Rector and Dean for the longest time on record, 61 years. When he died in 1906, within a few days of his 93rd birthday, he had been for several years the oldest beneficed clergyman in Essex, if not in the whole country.

A son of Sir Edmund Carrington, the first Chief Justice of Ceylon, the new Dean was a French scholar and a poet of some repute. Some people considered him far too wrapped up in his poetical studies (which included published translations of Hugo and Baudelaire and also an anthology of French poetry), a gentle dreamer not well suited to the work of a parish priest. He had been educated at Charterhouse and Caius College, Cambridge, and had married a niece of the Dean of Canterbury, Miss Juanita Lyall. By all accounts she was a strange person, and there were many weird stories about her, most of them probably unfounded, whispered in the parish. For one thing, she rarely went to church and was hardly ever seen about the district, although she welcomed visitors who called at the Deanery. It was said that she was extremely passionate; that she used to beat her three daughters unmercifully; that it was she who chose the curates, invariably taking the cheapest she could get to fill the post. Towards the end of the Dean's life it was generally acknowledged that Mrs. Carrington ran the parish; in the words of the late Mr. Alfred Hills, 'she used to rule the roost at Parish Meetings and so on'. When any document was brought to the Deanery for the Dean's signature, she would take the paper out of the room, sign it herself and then bring it back. With practice she must have become adept at forging her husband's writing!

The Carringtons did not much care for the English climate, and they spent a good deal of their time abroad, so that for much of the year the parish was left in the haphazard care of the curates. Under the terms of his commission, the Dean was free to engage whom he chose, and the curates did not require a licence from the diocesan Bishop. He—or his wife—certainly appear to have made some odd appointments, and there was a constant succession of new men. It used to be a regular game among the younger members of the congregation to compete against one another to see who could remember the greater number and the most extraordinary. The stories never failed to amuse.

There was one unfortunate by the name of Squib, a bachelor and an ugly, thin man with hair on his face, who laboured under the delusion that all the local young ladies had designs on him. 'It has pleased the Almighty to give to me the greatest blessing that it is possible to confer upon man, I have no desire to marry', he is said to have announced from the pulpit one Sunday. It is unlikely that any hearts were broken.

Another used to preach the most remarkable sermons in which he took each of the 'villains' of the Bible in turn and tried to prove what excellent characters they were; these were dubbed by the parish as his 'Sunday whitewash'.

Then there was one curate who used to turn up at church wearing hunting kit barely concealed under his surplice; it was well-known that this particular man had been discharged from Springfield Church for being drunk at early morning Communion. Another was sent to prison for nine months shortly after arrival in Bocking, convicted of 'an offence on a little girl at Church Street'. Yet another had to be rushed to a lunatic asylum. Not surprisingly, it all caused quite a scandal.

The Dean, when in residence, was in the habit of preaching excessively long sermons, usually delivered in a bored manner punctuated by sighs and a number of embarrassing pauses when he was unable to read his own writing. But when it came to reading the lessons, he would do this at such speed that the more mischievous members of the congregation called him 'Dean Swift'. Margaret Tabor, whose grandfather then owned Bocking Hall, remembered attending church service as a child and how the Dean would mount the pulpit in black gown and bright yellow gloves, which he would carefully adjust before he began to speak. In those days the Hall pew was what she called 'a sort of opera box in the chancel, entered by a private staircase from the North door',[72] which afforded a splendid view of everyone present. Near the South door there would be a huge basket piled high with loaves of bread, for distribution after the service.

For all their faults and their absences abroad, the Carringtons contributed generously to the material welfare of the parish and especially to the fabric of St. Mary's Church, to which little had been done to remedy the ravages of the Civil War period. A new organ, built by Norman and Beard, was installed in 1905. Other restoration work undertaken during Dean Carrington's time at Bocking included the re-casting of two bells, the seventh and the eighth, which was done in 1856, and the installation of new pews in about 1880 to replace the 'horsebox' type that had been put in at the beginning of the 19th century. These new pews were the work of a local carpenter, Samuel Parmenter, and the gift of Mr. William Walford, a member of one of the well-known local clothiers' families.

On Sunday, 13 December 1896 there was an alarming incident during Mattins when part of the roof near the east end of the nave began to collapse. The congregation were quickly evacuated, and the local builders, Parmenter and his men, summoned. Temporarily the falling timbers were propped up, and the following day the Diocesan surveyor came to inspect the damage. It was discovered that the ends of the main beams had decayed in the masonry and that the entire church roof, a considerable weight of lead, was on the point of crashing.

The surveyor came up with an ingenious scheme to save the roof: specially shaped steel girders were inserted into the masonry to support it, and the old nave timbers were bolted onto them, so that instead of these timbers carrying the weight of the lead roof, they were themselves supported by, or rather bolted to and hanging from, the steel girders. This work, together with the rebuilding of the chancel arch and minor repairs to the tower, chapels and vestry carried out at the same time cost a total of £741 16s. 4d. As soon as he heard what had happened, Dean Carrington, who was on one of his prolonged visits to Italy at the time, presumably to escape the English winter, sent a cheque for £100 to the restoration fund.

He also gave to the church the two windows in the clear-storey of the chancel, on the north side. One shows the blue-robed figure of his patron, Archbishop Howley, with the arms of the See of Canterbury impaling Howley and Howley impaling Capel; the other represents Sir Edmund Carrington in his red robes as Chief Justice of Ceylon, with the arms of Carrington impaling Belli (his wife's family) and Carrington impaling Capel.

Towards the end of his long life the Dean became an invalid and was no longer able to officiate in church. It was rumoured that he could not resign because he was unable to sign his name, and it must have been at about this time that his wife developed her skill! Almost his only pleasure was to drive out in his brougham, which he did nearly every day until a few days before his death, but he spoke to no one on these sorties and was often seen by his parishioners to be in tears.

Anniversaries are always an occasion for the church bells to be rung, and there was one special day at the beginning of Dean Carrington's term of office at Bocking which was remembered in the district for a long time. This was Friday, 26 June 1846, when the firm of Courtaulds declared a general holiday to celebrate the 21st year of their business. There was a procession of carriages and marchers through the streets, with a band playing, the bells ringing, as far as the meadow in front of Samuel Courtauld's house at High Garrett. Here a marquee for 2,000 people had been set up and there were the usual entertainments, followed in the evening by a dinner given by the workers to the Board.

There was another happy occasion early in February 1904, when the six bells of St. Mary's were rung to celebrate the Dean's 90th birthday. They were rung again at Easter that year in honour of the Dean's entering his 60th year of office, but this time it was a new peal. At her own expense Mrs. Carrington had had the bells re-hung and two new trebles added to make the octave. The first of these trebles is inscribed with the names of the Bocking ringers who rang the last peal on the six, and the first on the new eight. The second bears an inscription commemorating the event.

These bells were by no means the last gift of the Carrington family to the parish. One of the Dean's daughters—Evelyn, who married a wealthy Italian, Count Martinengo Cesaresco, in her turn left bequests to Bocking when she died abroad in 1932.

Henry Carrington died on 2 January 1906. His body lay in state in the Deanery library until the day of the funeral, when he was buried at Panfield. A memorial service was held at St. Mary's and afterwards the Bocking ringers rang a muffled peal.

900th Anniversary

On Sunday, 25 November 1906 the bells of the parish church and all other local churches rang to celebrate a great historical event: the 900th anniversary of the gift by Aetheric and Leofwyn of the church and lands at Bocking to Canterbury.

Special services were held, and Dean Brownrigg took as his text for the day, 'Thy truth also remaineth from one generation to another'. The Archbishop of Canterbury, Dr. Randall Davidson, wrote:

> The work for God which nine centuries have witnessed in such a parish is of paramount importance to the national life, and Bocking only affords a specimen of what has been, by God's grace, carried forward in other parishes throughout the land.

Bocking Deanery had long been one of the most valuable livings in the Archbishop's gift, and it is interesting to note that at the turn of the century it was listed in *Crockford's Clerical Directory* as being worth £880 gross per annum (£350 plus the house).

Peacocks and Rose Farthings

John Studholme Brownrigg came to the Deanery after 22 years as Secretary of the National Society. Born in Jamaica on 27 June 1841, the son of a general in the Grenadier Guards, the new Dean was a man of 65 at the time of his appointment. Educated at Eton and Magdalen College, Cambridge, he had been ordained in 1864, had served as a Canon of Bangor and was later made a Canon Emeritus. He was to follow in the Carrington tradition by living to a grand old age: he died on 15 October 1930, in his 90th year. Towards the end of his life he used to boast that he was the oldest Etonian alive.

On his arrival at Bocking in March 1906, Dean Brownrigg was upset to learn that the school had just been handed over to the Chelmsford Diocesan Board, and he made strenuous but abortive efforts to get it restored to local trustees. He was very interested in the history of the parish and the Deanery and made a point of reviving several old customs. He acquired the lordship of the manor and used to hold a manorial dinner once a year at which he delighted in dispensing food and drink with lavish hospitality. By all accounts he was a great humorist and was never at a loss for a witty story: a few of his more sober-minded parishioners were heard to say that the only time he was serious was in the pulpit.

The Dean was a familiar figure out and about in the parish and was a great favourite with the children, always carrying a

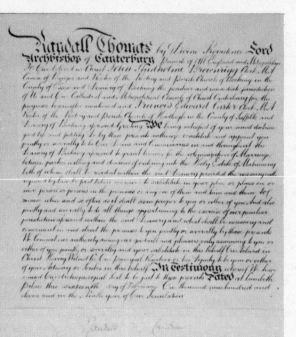

Fig. 11

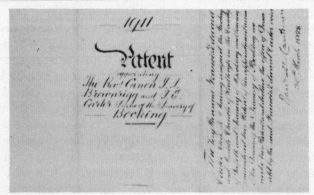

Fig. 12

bag of sweets in his pocket with which he regaled those he met on their way to or from the school. He was often to be seen driving in his old-fashioned yellow-painted horsedrawn cab, which he much prized, from the Deanery to Braintree railway station, where he caught the train to attend meetings in London. Unfortunately little else is remembered of his time at Bocking, although he was resident there for nearly a quarter of a century and his name is still spoken of with great affection. Certainly he added some colour to the Deanery scene, not only with his annual dinners but with half a dozen peacocks, of which he was especially proud. During the First World War the Dean used to claim that these birds seemed to know instinctively whenever Zeppelins were approaching and that they were far more reliable than any air raid siren.

Soon after the Brownriggs came to live at Bocking, the hideous Victorian cement casing was removed from the exterior of the Deanery. The transformation which its removal effected to the terrace side of the house is shown in an old picture postcard of *circa* 1890 and a snapshot taken much later, in 1958 (Pl. 25, 26).

Improvements made to the church at Dean Brownrigg's expense included electric lighting and new entrance gates. He was also instrumental in getting the choir stalls, the reredos and chancel screen installed and in instituting a surpliced choir.

The keeping of peacocks at the Deanery was only one of the traditions followed by the next occupant, Dean Edgar Rogers, who arrived in May 1931. He had four magnificent birds strutting about the lawns, including one particular favourite known to everyone as 'Peter'. All the peacocks died, however, one after the other, during the Second World War, largely as a result of feeding problems. The pigeons in the dovecote also disappeared during the war years, presumably eaten to supplement meagre meat rations, and were never replaced.

The other tradition maintained by Dean Rogers was his hobby of coin collecting. Mrs. R. H. Sawyer, his niece, who spent some time as a child at the Deanery, recalls that indoors there were 'books everywhere, and in the Dean's study coins spread out all over the floor'. One of seven children born into a wealthy fruit-broker's family in Liverpool, Edgar Rogers had been a Casherd scholar at St. John's College, Oxford, and he had read law at Magdalen before deciding on a career in the Church. As well as a history of the Early English Church, he had published several works on old coinage. He was a Fellow of the Society of Antiquaries and was well-known in numismatic circles for his collections of ancient Greek coins and of the celebrated 'Rose Farthings' issued during the reign of Charles I.

After a short spell as a curate in Wigan and eight years as vicar of one of the City of London's most historic parishes, St. Sephuchre's, Dr. Rogers had been appointed Chaplain General and Secretary of the Church Lads' Brigade, a post which he held from 1912 until 1931, when he came to Bocking. While with the Brigade he organised a Million Shilling Fund, which raised about £50,000. During the First World War he raised a battalion of King's Royal Rifles and was awarded an O.B.E. for his services.

A familiar figure in the neighbourhood, always clad in cassock and biretta, Dean Rogers naturally took a special interest in the youth of the parish. But he had a kind word for everyone, young and old alike. He used to say that when he first came to Bocking the elderly members of his congregation all warned him that it was his solemn duty to live to ninety! This, as it turned out, was one Deanery tradition he was unable to achieve, although he stubbornly stuck to the job (and that of Air Raid Warden) throughout the war years and until the autumn of 1954, when he was over eighty. It was during the Second World War that a bomb fell on the Deanery and demolished one of the big chimneys. Another notable wartime event was the collection and sale of old coins, war medals and decorations which the Dean organised with the help of his churchwarden, Mr. Harold Joyce; they raised £26,000 jointly for the British Red Cross Society and the Order of St. John of Jerusalem.

During Dean Rogers' incumbency more improvements were made to the church, the most important being the electrification of the organ, the restoration of the baptistry, the north and south chapel screens, and the setting up of the rood.

When the time came that he had to give up, a sale was held at the Deanery of many of his treasures, in order to provide for his retirement, and in November 1954 the Dean and Mrs. Rogers went to live in Gloucestershire, where he died in 1961. His departure from Bocking marked the end of a chapter in the history of the Deanery, for he was the last in a long line of 'scholar Deans', although not quite the last Dean to reside in the old house.

Recent Incumbents

Bocking developed very rapidly after the war. The expansion of Courtaulds created a need for more labour and so for more housing. Some of the old clothiers' houses were pulled down, and much of the town's character went with them.

Life was also changing at the Deanery. The modern incumbent, no longer a man of substantial private means, could not afford to live in the style of his predecessors, nor did he wish to do so. Even if he had been able to afford it, he would not have found the staff needed to run the large house and garden. Canon H. D. S. Bowen, who lived there as Dean from 1955 until 1963, did his best, but inevitably the old standards could not be kept up and economies had to be made. It followed that the property was in some measure neglected, and the house fell into serious disrepair. Within a short time of the appointment of the present Dean, the Very Reverend Kenneth E. Wade, it was realised that the Deanery required many thousands of pounds to be spent on it, and after much careful consideration a decision was taken by the Church Commissioners to dispose of the house and garden, retaining a plot of land on the brow of the hill (the site of the former Glebe Farm, which was burned down in 1921) on which to build a more convenient modern house for the Dean and Rector. The necessary deeds were drawn up, and the house known for some 400 years as 'Bocking Deanery' became, at the stroke of a pen, 'The Old Deanery, Bocking'.

A thousand years had passed since Aetheric made his Will bequeathing that hide of land to 'the priest who serves God there'.

POSTSCRIPT

The Deanery story does not end there. Ambitious plans were evolved by the new owners, in which Mr. A. E. Evans was the prime mover: experts were called in, and no money was spared in devising plans to restore the property inside and out. Excitement mounted as the work of demolishing the Victorian additions and stripping down to the old Tudor framework progressed. Fragments of the house's chequered history were revealed one by one: some Tudor wall decoration on the first floor; unique medieval craftsmanship in the roof-timbers; the priest's hole in the attic at the top of the stairs which had been known to exist for over a century. It was then that the idea was first conceived of compiling and preserving in a permanent form, for the enjoyment of future visitors to the house, a record of Bocking Deanery and of the people who had lived there through the centuries.

That Mr. Evans's admirable scheme failed to come to fruition, and that while this book has been in preparation the Old Deanery again changed hands, is already history. Now it is a family home that echoes with the laughter and merry chatter of vivacious children. What happens next, although the Royal guests and peacocks and manorial dinners are no more, will also one day be history—even, perhaps, another book.

REFERENCES AND NOTES

Where a work is listed in the bibliography, only the surname of the author and the short title are given in this section. Abbreviations used are:—

Canterbury	..	Cathedral Library and Archives, Canterbury.
E.R.O.	..	Essex Record Office, Chelmsford
Lambeth	..	Lambeth Palace Library, London.
P.R.O.	..	Public Record Office, London.

1. Whitelock, *English Historical Documents*, I, pp. 293-7.

2. A measure of land, originally sufficient for a peasant household, but which varied in different parts of the country.

3. Undated, but probably 961-995. Canterbury, *Chartae Antiquae* B.2; translation by Whitelock, *Anglo-Saxon Wills*, p. 43.

4. Undated, but historians now agree it to be not earlier than 995 and not later than 999. Canterbury, *Chartae Antiquae* B.1; translation by Whitelock, *op. cit.* pp. 45-7.

N.B.—Both charters B.1 and B.2 are endorsed with the date 997: Whitelock considers the endorsement of Aetheric's Will in a 13th-century hand to be wrong, but 997 is probably correct for Ethelred's confirmation charter.

5. Lambeth, MS. 303 f. 115.

6. Canterbury, Register P. 170/171.

7. Canterbury, *Chartae Antiquae* B.255.

8. Translation taken from *Victoria County History: Essex*, I (1903), p. 436. The comparison is with the time of Edward the Confessor at the date of January 1066.

9. For an account of these offences in Essex Archdeacons' Courts, *see* F. G. Emmison, *Elizabethan Life: Morals and the Church Courts*, 1973.

10. The Dean and Rector of Bocking is appointed by the Archbishop of Canterbury, whereas the present Rector of Hadleigh was appointed by the Bishop of Bury St. Edmunds. When a Dean and Rector of Bocking dies or vacates his office, two new Deans have to be commissioned, and in the meantime the incumbent of Hadleigh reverts to the style of 'Rector' only.

11. Taken from an undated agrarian survey, catalogued as late 13th century. Canterbury, Register R.E.105. Quoted by Nichols, *Custodia Essexae*, V, p. 13.

12. Canterbury, Register W.14.

13. P.R.O., Court Rolls, bundle 11, Nos. 2, 12, 25, 29.

14. *Ibid.*, No. 7.

15. Canterbury, *Chartae Antiquae* B.36.

16. The 60-year lease granted to Doreward by the Prior of Christ Church in 1346 is in Canterbury, *Chartae Antiquae* B.233a.

17. Canterbury, Register S, ff. 428/9.

18. Communicants, or those over 14 years of age. Morant, *History and Antiquities of the County of Essex,* II, p. 389.

18a. *Calendar of State Papers, Foreign and Domestic, Henry VIII,* 1540, Vol. XV, p. 476.

19. *Acts of the Privy Council,* 1550-1552, pp. 198-9.

20. Strype, *Life and Acts of Matthew Parker,* pp. 303-7.

21. Quoted from manuscript notes by Canon H. D. S. Bowen, Dean of Bocking, 1955-63. No sources given.

22. *Idem.*

23. *Idem.*

24. *Idem.*

25. P.R.O., Prob. 23/31.

26. Canterbury, Register W.15.

27. *Ibid.*

28. *Calendar of Essex Sessions,* E.R.O., Q/SR/145/2a. The bishop was John Sterne, Suffragan Bishop of Colchester, Vicar of Witham and a J.P.

29. E.R.O., T/Z 20. Mr. Alfred Hills, M.A., F.S.A., of the 'Old House', Bradford Street, Bocking, a local solicitor and antiquary. He gave his collection to the Essex County Council before his death in 1952.

30. Letter from Earl of Warwick to the Secretary of State, 27 July 1640, *Calendar of State Papers, Domestic, Charles I,* Vol. XVI, pp. 517-8.

31. *See* F. G. Emmison, *Early Town Meetings: Braintree and Finchingfield* (1970).

32. E.R.O., Q/SR/266/121.

33. Quoted by Addison, *Essex Heyday,* pp. 134-7. *See also Acts of the Privy Council, 1629-30,* pp. 24-5.

34. Walker, *A True Account of the Author of a Book entitled Eikon Basilike,* published in 1629 (after his death).

35. Lambeth, Comm. XIIa/8 ff. 286-8. Translation taken from the papers of the late Mr. Alfred Hills.

36. Page, ed., *Essex in the Days of Old,* pp. 105-18.

37. B.M., 816m 14 (46).

38. Wordsworth, *King Charles I, the author of Icon Basilike* (1828) and *Who wrote Eikon Basilike?* (1824).

39. Walker, *op. cit.* (See note 34).

40. Quoted by Bowen in manuscript notes. No source given.

41. *Idem.*

42. Gilbert Burnet (1643-1715), Bishop of Salisbury, *History of His Own Time,* I (Oxford, 1823), pp. 87-8.

43. The first register of St. Mary's, Bocking, 1558-1639, was privately printed in 50 copies by J. J. Goodwin of Hartford, Conn., U.S.A., 1903. A copy is at the Essex Record Office.

44. P.R.O., Prob. 11/346.

45. Addison, *Essex Heyday,* p. 175; Hills, in 'Bunyan at Bocking', *Essex Review,* 38 (1929), pp. 1-9.

46. In 1974 two further bells were added to the Bocking peal, named 'Frederick' and 'Augustine' after Frederick Bearman and Augustine Courtauld.

47. Percy, 'Anecdotes of the Pulpit', under Dawes (p. 283 in 1870 edition).

48. *Ibid.*

49. Until 1752 the Old Style calendar was in use in England, the year beginning on 25 March and not 1 January.

50. Dean Walkers's notebooks are in the possession of the present Dean and Rector of Bocking, The Very Reverend Kenneth E. Wade. Photocopies are at the Essex Record Office, T/A 433/2-3.

51. No relation to the previous Dean of Bocking, so far as is known.

52. 1 pole = 30¼ sq. yds. (272¼ sq. ft.). 40 poles = 1 rood. 4 roods = 1 acre.

53. Bowen, 'Notebooks of a Curate of Bocking 1737-1770', in *Essex Review*, 258 (1957), pp. 19-23.

54. Notebook started by Dean Wordsworth in 1816, listing charities given to the parish, and added to by later Deans. In the possession of the present Dean and Rector of Bocking, The Very Reverend Kenneth E. Wade.

55. E.R.O., D/APb W2/10.

56. E.R.O., D/P 268/14.

57. E.R.O., D/P 268/18/2.

58. E.R.O., D/DCd Z7.

59. Quoted by Watson, *Mary Russell Mitford*, pp. 17-18.

60. Quoted by Hill, *Mary Russell Mitford and Her Surroundings*, Chapter XIV. See also *Braintree and Witham Times*, 24 November 1932.

61. From private papers belonging to Mr. Rowland Oakeley.

62. Robinson, *On Books and their Writers*, ed. Edith J. Morley (1938), I, p. 131.

63. Overton and Wordsworth, *Christopher Wordsworth, Bishop of Lincoln*, p. 9.

64. See note 54.

65. Quoted in *Essex Review*, III, No. 12 (October 1894).

66. Overton and Wordsworth, *op. cit.*, p. 8.

67. Wordsworth, *Annals of My Early Life*, Chapter I.

68. P.R.O., Prob. 11/1831.

69. From private papers in the possession of Mr. Rowland Oakeley.

70. *Idem.*

71. *Idem.*

72. Tabor, 'Bocking Church', typescript article in the possession of the present Dean and Rector of Bocking, The Very Reverend Kenneth E. Wade.

BIBLIOGRAPHY

General Sources

William Addison, *Essex Heyday* (1949).
Calendar of State Papers, Domestic, Charles I, 1640, Vol. XVI.
Frederic Chancellor, *Ancient Sepulchral Monuments of Essex* (1890).
Irene J. Churchill, *Canterbury Administration* (1933).
Crockford's Clerical Directory (first published 1858), various dates.
Dictionary of National Biography.
C. R. Hart, *The Early Charters of Eastern England* (Leicester, 1966).
Philip Morant, *The History and Antiquities of the County of Essex* (1768).
R. Newcourt, *Repertorium Ecclesiasticum,* Vol. II (1710).
Dorothy M. Owen, *The Records of the Established Church in England* (1970).
Royal Commission on Historical Monuments: Essex, Vol. I (1916).
P. H. Sawyer, *Anglo-Saxon Charters,* Royal Historical Society (1968).
John Strype, *The Life and Acts of Matthew Parker, Archbishop of Canterbury* (1711).
Victoria County History: Essex, 5 vols (London and Oxford, 1903-56).
Trudy West, *The Timber-frame House in England* (Newton Abbott, 1970).
Dorothy Whitelock, *Anglo-Saxon Wills* (Cambridge, 1930). *English Historical Documents, c. 500-1042* (Cambridge, 1955).
Thomas Wright, *History and Topography of the County of Essex,* 2 vols. (1836).

Local and Secondary Sources

H. D. S. Bowen, 'Notebooks of a Curate of Bocking 1737-1770', in *Essex Review,* 258 (1957), pp. 19-23.
Hugh Chapman, *St. Mary's Deanery Church, Bocking* (pamphlet guide) (1954).
Andrew Clark, 'A Bocking Bread Charity 1605-1784', in *Essex Review,* 26 (1917), pp. 6-11.
M. Cunnington and S. A. Warner, *Braintree and Bocking* (1906).
William Gilbert, 'Token Coinage of Essex in the Seventeenth Century', in *Transactions of the Essex Archaeological Society,* XIII (1915), pp. 190-1.
J. J. Goodwin, *Register of St. Mary's Church, Bocking, 1558-1639,* privately printed (Essex Archaeological Society, 1903) (copies at Essex Record Office and in the possession of The Very Reverend Kenneth E. Wade, Dean and Rector of Bocking).
'Heraldic Activity in Essex' (anonymous article), *Essex Review,* 35 (1926), pp. 150-6.
Alfred Hills, 'The Arms of Bocking'; 'Bunyan at Bocking'; 'Deans and Coins'; 'Tales of Bocking'; some reprinted from *Essex Review,* deposited together with other papers at the E.R.O. (T/Z 20); also 'St. Mary's, Bocking', typescript in the possession of The Very Reverend Kenneth E. Wade, Dean and Rector of Bocking.

John F. Nichols, *Custodia Essexae, A Study of the Conventual Property held by the Priory of Christ Church, Canterbury, in the Counties of Essex, Suffolk and Norfolk,* unpublished University of London Ph.D. thesis, 1930, presented to the Essex Record Office.

T. Rayner, *History of the Bocking Cloth Industry,* unpublished typescript written *c.* 1950-55, deposited at the Essex Record Office (T/Z 27).

Margaret Tabor, 'Bocking Church', typescript in the possession of The Very Reverend Kenneth E. Wade, Dean and Rector of Bocking.

John Walker, Notebooks, in the possession of the present Dean (photocopies at Essex Record Office, T/A 433 2-3).

C. H. Ward-Jackson, *A History of Courtaulds,* printed for private circulation (1941).

Additional Biographical Sources used

On Dr. John Barkham:

J. G. Milne, 'A Bocking Dean and his Coins', in *Essex Review*, 42 (1933), pp. 122-4.

Harold Smith, 'Rowdy Soldiers, July 1640', in 'Notes and Queries', *Essex Review*, 37 (1928), p. 143.

On Sir William Dawes:

R. and S. Percy, 'Anecdotes of the Pulpit', in *The Percy Anecdotes*, 4 vols. (1820-3).

On Dr. John Gauden:

Anthony Walker, *A True Account of the Author of a Book entitled Eikon Basilike* (1692).

C. Walters, 'The Notorious Dean of Bocking and the "Eikon Basilike"', in John T. Page, ed., *Essex in the Days of Old* (1898).

Christopher Wordsworth, *King Charles I the Author of Icon Basilike* (1828). *Who wrote Eikon Basilike?* (1824).

On the Murray-Aynsley and Oakeley families:

The Hon. Mrs. Francis Drummond, *Some Notes relating to the Life of Sir Herbert Oakeley, 3rd Baronet,* printed for private circulation (1892).

Constance Hill, *Mary Russell Mitford and her Surroundings* (1920).

E. F. Oakeley, *The Oakeley Pedigree,* printed for private circulation (1934).

Vera Watson, *Mary Russell Mitford* (1949).

On Dr. Christopher Wordsworth and his wife:

H. Crabb Robinson (ed. Edith J. Morley), *Correspondence with the Wordsworth Circle* (Oxford, 1927).

E. V. Lucas, *Charles Lamb and the Lloyds* (1898).

J. H. Overton and E. Wordsworth, *Christopher Wordsworth, Bishop of Lincoln* (1890).

Charles Wordsworth, *Annals of my Early Life* (1891).

INDEX